S0-AGV-539

The Resurrection Life

The Power of Jesus
for Today

The Resurrection Life

The Power of Jesus
for Today

Dr. Myron S. Augsburger

Evangel Publishing House

Nappanee, Indiana 46550

The Resurrection Life: The Power of Jesus for Today
Copyright © 2005 by Myron Augsburger

Requests for information should be addressed to:
Evangel Publishing House
2000 Evangel Way
P.O. Box 189
Nappanee, Indiana 46550
Phone: (800) 253-9315
Internet: www.evangelpublishing.com

Unless otherwise noted, Bible references are primarily from the New Revised Standard or King James versions.

All rights reserved. No part of this publication may be reproduced, stored in a retrieval system, or transmitted in any form or by any means–electronic, mechanical, photocopy, recording, or any other–except for brief quotations in printed reviews, without the prior permission of Evangel Publishing House, P.O. Box 189, Nappanee, Indiana 46550.

Edited by Kathy Borsa
Cover Design by Jeffrey Hall, ION Graphic Design Works

ISBN: 1-928915-71-X
Library of Congress Catalog Card Number: 2005930301

Printed in the United States of America

5 6 7 8 9 EP 8 7 6 5 4 3 2

DEDICATION

I am personally thankful to the church for its wonderful heritage of faith and for the fellowship in Christ that holds me accountable. My gratitude also to many persons through whom the Spirit has enriched my life, especially to my wife, Esther, and to our children. Esther and I have walked together for 55 years and we delight together in the Lord. I am grateful to Esther for her help with this book. She was a great help in making the ideas flow clearly. I also want to give special recognition to Melodie Davis for her editorial expertise, which markedly improved this work.

TABLE OF CONTENTS

INTRODUCTION

"The third day he rose again from the dead, he ascended into heaven and sits on the right hand of God the Father Almighty, from thence he shall come again to judge the quick and the dead" (from the *Apostle's Creed*).

For centuries Christians have recited and claimed to believe the above phrase found in the *Apostle's Creed*. As Christians, do we really understand what we are saying—let alone begin to really live it?

In this post-modern twenty-first century, we desperately need fresh insight into the workings of our sovereign God. We need to acknowledge Him but also recognize the manner in which He is at work. We should not seek to understand His movement by our patterns or with our preferences but in ways that are consistent with God himself. Our place must be seen primarily in relation to how we as a Church, and to some degree as Nations, can be His agents in advancing His purpose in and for the world community.

By faith we affirm that Christ lives! He is sovereign Lord, at God's right hand, and in relationship with Christ, we live too! How very significant in these turbulent days. We celebrate the fact of Christ's Resurrection, which is affirmed by historical accounts. We celebrate this fact with assurance because of His work among us as Lord of the universe. The reality of the Resurrection creates a new order of life—a covenant of freedom in Christ.

So we must ask ourselves, in what way is the power of His Resurrection current to us who believe? The dynamic of God's love enables us to live a new life in transforming grace allowing us to share in a new community. This is a new quality of life, for grace is not only forgiveness and acceptance, but God's grace is also transforming. To celebrate God's grace is not escapism from real life. There is healing therapy in this grace that allows us to change our lives enabling us to live as disciples of a risen Christ.

Furthermore, we need to fully participate in covenant with the risen Lord. Without a sense of what this covenant truly provides and requires, we will not be able to function as disciples in this post-modern age. Only by fellowship with Him can we be free from a mere cultural form of religion. To be conformed to the order of His kingdom we need a sense of accountability to the risen Christ. The power for our transformation from individualism and therefore, for community, comes from sharing in the freedom provided by His Resurrection.

Scripture claims that the tomb is empty and that Jesus did rise from the dead. Scripture also tells us that the disciples and many other believers saw Him. In fact, five hundred people saw Him at the same time! While it may be said that we cannot prove the Resurrection of Christ, we recognize the claim that He rose from the dead is itself historical. The same factual documents that relate everything else about Jesus also relate His Resurrection. History proclaims the disciples believed that Jesus had risen from the dead. The disciples did not create the resurrection—the Resurrection created the disciples. It is this knowledge that makes us free!

This book emphasizes the transforming power of the Resurrection, which strengthens and prepares us for authentic Christian living. He rose, He ascended, and He is enthroned at God's right hand. It is the Resurrection of Christ that undergirds all other areas of our faith. Identification with the risen Christ means to take one's place in His community and to walk with Him in daily life. My writing of this book is both an interpretation and a confession, for I have not yet achieved the level of victory and holiness to which I aspire. I can only rest in His grace of acceptance. Christ enables me to claim His

Resurrection power as honestly as I can. I commit to the discipleship of walking with the Master, seeking to follow Him daily.

The New Testament is a vital witness to the person and life of
Jesus Christ. It confirms Jesus as being the seed of David in fulfillment of the Old Testament promise of Christ's coming. It
also tells us that Christ's Resurrection is evidence of His being
the Son of God (Romans 1:3-4). Further, His life was the declaration of authentic humanness. His Resurrection is the declaration that in our humanness we can participate in fellowship with
the eternal God. He lived and taught the will of God. This is
our narrative as believers. It is the story of faith in action. Our
life of faith is a journey in grace—the grace of His acceptance
of us in spite of our limitations.

In light of this stupendous fact we must then ask, what does
it mean to know Jesus? Does this mean to know the historical
facts? Is it a reference to some inner feeling of having Jesus in
one's heart? To know Him as a living sovereign Lord at God's
right hand present by His Spirit in our experience does mean
knowing Him at the very heart of one's life. It also means we
know Him as a historical person as well. Knowing Him histori-
cally, greatly improves our ability to know Him as a contemporary with whom we walk day by day.

We have head knowledge "about Jesus" from the study of the
historical person and heart knowledge "of Jesus" through our
faith relationship. Faith moves us from thinking about God to
thinking *with* God. Our faith, while personal, is not private or
individualistic. It [faith] incorporates us into His community.
Our faith, above all, is about a relationship and not simply
philosophical. The church is also intended to be a relational
community, not a corporation or institution as such.

We must learn to confess a relationship with Christ that
affects our behavior. We must take the historical Jesus and His
teachings seriously as a pattern for life. Jesus is our teacher, our
mentor, as well as our redeemer (1 Peter 2:21). Some contempo-

rary Christians build systems of faith and/or ethics by lifting values from Jesus but not identifying with Him or walking with Him in life. Others fail to emphasize and follow His teachings. When we follow His teachings, it is the highest affirmation of His person and of the higher ethic. Faith is not primarily about ideas or values. It must be placed in relationship with God, in solidarity with Christ, and with the community of believers.

Our highest loyalty is to the risen Lord, to live by the new life in which He has engaged us. This means to live in awareness that there are two kingdoms and two loyalties. Our highest accountability is to the kingdom of God, which shapes the new community in following Christ.

Myron S. Augsburger

1

What Happens Because of the Resurrection?

"The gospel he promised beforehand through his prophets in the Holy Scriptures regarding his Son, who as to his human nature was a descendent of David, and who through the Spirit of holiness was declared with power to be the Son of God, by his Resurrection from the dead: Jesus Christ our Lord" (Romans 1:2-4).

"Therefore we have been buried with him by baptism into death, so that, just as Christ was raised from the dead by the glory of the Father, so we too might walk in newness of life" (Romans 6:4).

"You hath he quickened who were dead in trespasses and sins...God, who is rich in mercy, for his great love wherewith he loved us, has now quickened us in Christ...for by grace you are saved" (Ephesians 2:1,3).

"Since, then, you have been raised with Christ, set your hearts on things above, where Christ is seated at the right hand of God. Set your minds on things above, not on earthly things. For you died, and your life is now hidden with Christ in God. When Christ, who is your life, appears, then you also will appear with him in glory" (Colossians 3:1-4).

Our Lord is sovereign, but He is neither invasive nor oppressive. He is simply there for each of us who will allow Him. His first expression is to love us—not to prove himself to us. God gives himself in love to the world, and in Jesus He gave himself fully. In the Resurrection, He assures us that the act of self-giving love is the act of a sovereign Lord—victor even over death. The passages of Scripture at the beginning of this chapter express the transforming nature of a resurrection gospel. The Resurrection is grace shining like a light into the darkness of human experience.

God's work of grace makes new creatures of all who believe. He begins by changing people not by changing circumstances. This new community is a different lifestyle, a new order of life together, and a new spirit for living. This, in turn, changes society as we walk with Christ in the journey of life. Remarkably, this newness is not tied to our achievements or our education but to faith. The average person of very simple faith enters into the richness of God's grace.

Allow me to share with you a courtroom scene that took place a few years ago in South Africa:

> A frail black woman, over 70 years old, stands to her feet. Facing her across the room are several white police officers, one of whom—Mr. van der Broek, has just been tried and found guilty of being implicated in the murders of both her son and her husband.
>
> A few years before Mr. van der Broek had come to the woman's home and taken her son, shot him at point-blank range and burned his body on a fire while van der Broek and his fellow officers partied. Several years later he and his cohorts returned and took away her husband.

For nearly two years she heard nothing and then Mr. van der Broek returned and took her to a place beside a river where she was shown her husband, bound and beaten, but still strong in spirit, lying on a pile of wood. The last words she heard her beloved husband speak as they poured gasoline over his body and set him aflame were, "Father, forgive them."

Now the woman stood in the courtroom and listened to the confessions offered by Mr. van der Broek. A member of South Africa's Truth and Reconciliation Commission turned to her and asked, "So what do you want? How should justice be delivered?"

"I want three things," the elderly woman said calmly but confidently. "I want first to be taken to the place where my husband's body was burned so that I can gather up the dust and give his remains a decent burial."

She continued, "My husband and son were my only family. I want secondly, therefore, for Mr. van der Broek to become my son. I would like for him to come twice a month to the ghetto and spend a day with me so that I can pour out on him whatever love I still have remaining within me."

"And finally, I want a third thing. I would like Mr. van der Broek to know that I offer him my forgiveness because Jesus Christ died to forgive. This was also the wish of my husband. And so, I would kindly ask someone to come to my side and lead me across the courtroom so that I can take Mr. van der Broek in my arms, embrace him and let him know that he is truly forgiven."

As the court assistants came to lead the elderly woman across the room, Mr. van der Broek was so overwhelmed that he fainted. Friends, family, neighbors—all victims of decades of oppression and injustice—began to sing softly but assuredly, "Amazing grace, how sweet the sound that saved a wretch like me." (Reported by James R. Krabill, Mennonite Church Peace and Justice Committee newsletter, June 1999.)

This is resurrection power empowering us to walk with God here and now. By His Resurrection—through grace—we are enabled to rise above the death-dealing impact of sin. That is, we can live joyously and victoriously by sharing in this self-giving love. This is a transforming covenant and community of mutuality. There are, however, questions that confront us, pointing beyond our present situation. Is the life we know here in this world all that there is? Were we created just for one world or for two? How does the other world overlap this one? And what are we to make of all of the ideas in various religions that humanity is immortal?

In our secular and humanistic culture, the understanding of God and His purpose for humanity is relegated to religious superstition. Any perception of the eternal dimensions of life is often dismissed as wishful thinking. But one of the great philosophers of ethics and religious thought, Emmanuel Kant, held that we must be immortal because the human mind has too much potential to be fulfilled in a mere lifetime of seventy years. Eastern religions have projected reincarnation to extend our lives into another cycle. But in the New Testament, Paul writes that Jesus brought "life and immortality to light through the gospel" (2 Timothy 1:10), and sets this in the context of the stupendous reality of the Resurrection.

Jesus taught a much larger life through a promise of resurrection. This is a unique form of immortality. The resurrection is more than a Greek or Eastern concept of immortality. We will actually live again. Jesus said, "He that lives and believes in me, though He were dead, yet shall He live." Believing in Him is to share deep togetherness with Him now and walk in newness of life. This brings a quality of life in which we are completely free—an introduction to the eternal reality. Fifty billion years from now we, as believers, expect to be still walking with God.

Since the resurrection of Christ means that He is living at God's right hand, ruling now in a kingdom of the Spirit, a very real concern is how we as believers can consciously recognize His presence. How do we share this Resurrection power in life today? Christian faith centered in the risen Christ means that we belong to Him (Romans 1:6). How do we open our lives intimately to Him today? To love Him should be understood first as meaning to open our lives personally, intimately, to Him. Further, the Resurrection means that He is the authority for our life pattern, for He is the One who made the will of God known in His earthly sojourn. Therefore He as Lord is our model for life. Christian faith is to walk with and to identify with Christ as we have come to know Jesus, the one true human person. This walk together is the dynamic of community.

Jesus said that the first of God's commandments is simply that we love Him. In a paraphrase of St. Augustine: We are not what we think or believe, but we are what we love. But how does one enter into the love of Jesus? An answer may be found when we understand love, not so much as a feeling but as an opening of one's life to another. While it is less easy to love some figure in past history it is altogether a different experience to love someone who is alive—a contemporary. This is a reality when we are in a relationship with the risen Lord, our contemporary. We are in love! The resurrection of Christ, then, is the essential precondition for a loving relation between our Lord and us. The nature of a living faith is solidarity with Him, identity with Him, opening our lives to Him. We moderns need this sense of immediacy, to move beyond a concept to a relationship. He is present in the world calling us to respond to Him.

In the quest of faith we not only ask, how can I come to know Jesus, but how do I know Jesus [now]? Do I know Him only as a person from the past who has had a major influence on life? As a holy man? As a prophet among prophets? As an example of the best in humanness? Or, do I know Him as my Redeemer, my risen Lord, my contemporary? In knowing and confessing Him as Lord do I then express His Lordship and my love by taking my place as His disciple and His servant?

Some years ago, the famous Oxford atheist Dr. Jonathan Glover gave a lecture on his position of atheism, claiming that we cannot know God. At the conclusion of his arguments a man arose with a question: "Dr. Glover, suppose that you were driving through a very difficult section of the city late at night when something goes wrong with your car and it stops in the middle of the street. You open the bonnet [hood] and are looking helplessly at the motor. Suddenly the door of a house across the street opens, and eight big fellows come out of the house and begin walking toward you. Would it make any difference to you if you knew that they were coming from a prayer meeting?" His response was an honest admission that there would be a very real difference.

Being a Christian is not simply having a conceptual belief in Jesus for at best our concepts are limited. Just as is true in our human relationships, belief in Jesus is identifying with Him and walking with Him as risen Jesus in one's life. True faith is a covenant relationship with Jesus. Faith is identification with Him, it is living with the verbal confession, "Christ is my Lord!" In this identification we can live by the power of the Spirit that raised Jesus from the dead. Such faith changes life by its focus on the person of Christ and on the spiritual dimensions of life.

And this is a simple faith relationship. The late Dr. John Harper, once president of the University of Chicago, said, "Why didn't someone tell me that I could become a Christian first and settle doubts later?" We relate to God without having all of our questions about God fully answered. Life has many issues that are not clearly answered, but we move by evidence that supports our faith. When we want to know God, want God to be God in our lives, we come to *Him,* not simply to a religion. In faith, we follow the evidence that God is present with us. We continue to ask questions about the mysteries of life and the awesome mystery of God. We do not deny honest doubt, but the function of doubt is to stimulate our quest for more evidence for a faith response. As Anselm of the twelfth century said of this freedom, "Faith seeks understanding."

The resurrection of Christ Jesus is unique to the Christian faith. Our belief is a faith response to the evidence of the empty tomb, a faith response to the witness of the disciples, of having seen the risen Christ and of the change in their lives. We also have the evidence that this Resurrection power has changed believer's lives through the centuries. Along with you, I have seen God at work transforming lives today, a transformation that we each need and which happens by the power of the Spirit. As G. K. Chesterton once said, "We need change—for whatever else is true of man, man isn't what he was meant to be." Our turbulent world is evidence of this fact.

Some key affirmations regarding the Resurrection: in thinking of His Resurrection we are confronted with the fact that the resurrection of Jesus happened in this world! The affirmation of the New Testament is that Jesus of Nazareth, who died on the cross, is resurrected and was seen by His disciples and by a multitude of believers in this world. For us to believe in the Incarnation is to say that God actually engaged humanness in Jesus; to believe in His Resurrection is to recognize that His engagement with humanness is extended in the redemptive meaning of hope for the future (see 1 Corinthians 15). The Scripture claims that "this same Jesus" who lived and died experienced Resurrection in "this world" and then ascended to heaven binding the two worlds together.

Jesus is now in glory, "seated on the right hand of God the Father, Almighty, from thence He shall come to judge the quick and the dead" *(Apostle's Creed)*. The resurrection of Christ is the revolutionary center of the gospel, for "He was delivered for our offenses, but raised again for our justification" (Romans 4:24). We stand in a long line representing followers of Jesus and it is this faith we now interpret in a secular 21st century.

There are themes in this book that I have treated in some of my other writings, on reconciliation, discipleship, and the work of the Holy Spirit. In this book I am focusing particularly on the freedoms of the Resurrection and the meaning this brings to such themes as the Atonement, reconciliation, salvation, discipleship, community, ethics, and futurism.

First, let's ask, what does it mean for me to live in a world where Christ is risen; where He is exalted at God's right hand; where He is Lord and sovereign; further, where He gives His Spirit; where He is head of the Church, a new community. Again, where He is the ultimate and universal "right," where He is the final judge of the entire world? This is a long and powerful list! There is special significance in seeing the Resurrection as an extension of the Incarnation, the extension of God's participation in humanness. We affirm with Calvin "He took humanity to heaven as the guarantee that we can be there some day." The Resurrection means that we think of Jesus as the one who was "declared with power to be the Son of God" as Paul says in Romans 1:4. At Pentecost Peter said, "God has raised this Jesus to life, and we are all witnesses of the fact. Exalted to the right hand of God, He has received from the Father the promised Holy Spirit and has now poured out what you see and hear" (Acts 2:32-33).

Secondly, the resurrection of Jesus has implications for our understanding of humanness extended beyond our current experience. It is our hope! His Resurrection is not to be thought of as some mystical or ghostly fantasy.

Christian experience is not a supernatural escape from the physical world. The resurrection of Jesus happened in this world of humanness. His appearance in form and substance was such that Mary at first mistook Him for another man. When two of His disciples met Him on the road to Emmaus, they met flesh and bones, not a ghost. He was real, they talked with Him as with any person, but incredulity kept them from recognizing Him until He had blessed the bread and departed.

The Resurrection happened in our sphere of life, in our world, and amidst our humanness. It was the work of our one God, now known as Father-Son-Holy Spirit, who acted to bring Jesus back to life. This is the same Jesus who before His death lived, taught and called us to the will of God. The disciples were told by the risen Jesus, "A spirit does not have flesh and bones as you see me have" (Luke 24:39). He was not an otherworldly spirit. His Resurrection is an extension of His life and presence and therefore of His teaching and calling.

Thirdly, the resurrection of Christ has significant hermeneutical implications. It is the key to our understanding His teachings as continuing His authority. In Ephesians, Paul writes that we have learned the way of Christ by the "truth as it is in Jesus" (4:20-21). That is, our understanding of Christ is tied to the life and teachings of Jesus. But we read Scripture not in a legalistic manner of values demanded of us but as a spirit of life shared with us. The Resurrection enables us to bridge from the teachings of the "earthly Jesus" to the "cosmic Christ." We should therefore not see a conflict between the teachings of Jesus about the kingdom of God and the teachings of the apostle Paul on being "in Christ" as Paul's focus is now relating with the risen Lord. There is no conflict when we view the gospel through the Resurrection, for Jesus Christ who announced the Gospel has *become* the Gospel. He has now become the "good news." Paul proclaimed the kingdom of God as actualized in the rule of this risen Lord, in Him the kingdom is the rule of God (see this in Paul, Acts 20:25, 28:23, 31; Romans 14:17; Colossians 1:13).

Actually Jesus already introduced this transition of thought in His words, "I confer on you a kingdom, just as my Father has conferred on me, so that you may eat and drink at my table in my kingdom" (Luke 22:28-29). Further, Paul interrelates the reconciling work of Christ, the experience of salvation, and the new life we enjoy in the victory of Christ (Romans 6:4-14) and our future hope. This hope for our future is specifically confirmed by the resurrection of Christ (1 Corinthians 15).

Fourth, the Resurrection is central in our understanding of Christian discipleship. In the exercise of faith, we join in solidarity with Jesus—with the risen Christ. Discipleship is relational; it is walking with Jesus in the Way. Discipleship is not a moralistic lifestyle; it is a fellowship with the living Christ. Paul refers to the fact that the same power that raised Christ from the dead is at work in us who believe (Ephesians 1:19-23). Again, the same power that raised Christ from the dead also quickens our mortal bodies by His Spirit who dwells in us (Romans 8:11). Discipleship is the recognition that Jesus is Lord and that the priorities of His kingdom are the pattern for our lives as disciples. We are citizens of heaven while living here in this world (Philippians 3:20), and we are "resident aliens" in society (see Hauerwaus and Willimon, *Resident Aliens*). Stanley Hauerwaus was quoted in *Time* magazine, saying, "If you use the word disciple you had better mean it!"

Much of my thinking about a resurrection Christology grows out of my study of the Anabaptist movement from the 16th century to the present. The Anabaptists not only saw the man Jesus as an example of the will of God and by His death our reconciliation with God, but they saw the risen Christ as our contemporary, as our companion, as our Lord. They were existentialists in their faith relationship. They spoke of sharing His Resurrection in a new life and of baptism being for those who "desire to walk in the resurrection of Jesus Christ and be buried with Him in death, so that they might rise with Him" (*Schleitheim Confession*, article 1).

As a continuum of this Anabaptist movement, the current "Confession of Faith in a Mennonite Perspective" makes a remarkable statement on the preceding point. "The church is called to witness to the reign of Christ by embodying Jesus' way in its own life and patterning itself after the reign of God. Thus it shows the world a sample of life under the lordship of Christ. "By its life, the church is to be a city on a hill, a light to the nations, testifying to the power of the resurrection by a way of life different from the societies around it" (MPH, Scottdale, PA, p. 42).

It is this walk in covenant, in community with Him, in solidarity with Christ that forms the ethical aspect of Christian discipleship. To walk in the resurrection of Jesus Christ is to live in relationship with Him as our risen Lord, to live by His teachings in and through His power. Resurrection freedom is sharing deliverance from the old life in which sin reigned and sharing the new life in which His Spirit reigns (Romans 6:6, see verses 4-14).

A unique witness to this faith in the Resurrection comes from a young man, Algerius of Naples, who studied at the University of Padua in the 16th century. There, in that turbulent time of religious conflict, through conversations on faith, Algerius became a believer in the Anabaptist sense and was baptized. Arrested for his faith he was taken to Venice and put on trial before the entire Senate. Since they were unable to dissuade him, he was sent to Rome to be further tested before the Pope himself. As he remained true to his faith he was condemned by the Council to die by burning at the stake. The account shows that he experienced horrible suffering, having boiling oil poured over his head and body until in rubbing his hand over his face the skin and hair came away! In sympathy, a Capuchin monk held a crucifix before Him, admonishing Him to engage its meaning, but Algerius pushed the crucifix away with the words of his prayer, "My Lord and God lives above in heaven...Pray tell me, in what manner I have deserved to be condemned? Is it that I have not answered the most illustrious senators, my lords, according to their pleasure? If I have said anything, it was not I at all that said it, since the Lord says that before the authorities it will not be us that speak, but the Spirit of our Father which will be in us Matthew 10:30" (quote from *Martyrs Mirror*, pp. 572, 573).

I tell this story to show how real the tensions were in the 16th century. But there have been many changes of relationship within the different expressions of the church through the centuries, especially since Vatican II and in various Protestant dialogues. But within the various expressions of the institutional church, there is general agreement on distinction made between those who only profess religion and those who identify with the Lord of whom religion should be witness. And even now, in the 21st century, in the conflict of religions, Christians frequently die for their faith in Christ as they witness to a relation with the Lord beyond religion itself. We worship Him, not just religious forms.

The Christian church, originally and through the centuries, has placed a strong emphasis on the Incarnation, on Jesus of Nazareth as the One in whom "the Word was made flesh and dwelled among us." This means that we should take most seriously His incarnate life as the expression of the will of God for our way of life. His teachings and mentoring are the pattern of life for us as disciples. Significantly we must understand the Resurrection as the extension or the continuation of the life of our Lord, for it is "this same Jesus" who lives now. This same Jesus appeared to Mary Magdalene in the garden and to His disciples before He ascended to God. The Resurrection extends his life and teachings for all time and eternity.

Too many Christians do not take seriously the normative aspects of the life of Jesus for Christian ethics. Philip Yancey's writing is something of an exception in his book, *The Jesus I Never Knew*, presenting the man Jesus, in a realistic way, the very human person who is our Savior. In the Anabaptist tradition the late John Howard Yoder's seminal work, *The Politics of Jesus*, is a theological reflection on taking the whole Jesus with utmost seriousness, as Redeemer but also as the norm for Christian ethics. A resurrection Christology offers a theological perspective that Jesus' life and ministry continue to be normative for discipleship.

From another tradition, Marcus Barth writes in a related manner of the Resurrection as validation of Christ's ministry: "The Resurrection is the enthronement of the divinely appointed intercessor for the sinners; it is the validation of his ministry; it is the proclamation of the work's accomplishment; it is the ground of all certainty and trust in the victory and regal rule of grace over sin" (*Acquittal By Resurrection*, Barth and Fletcher; Hold, Rinehart and Winston, N.Y. 1964, pp. 95-96).

As an Anabaptist/Mennonite, both by birth and by choice, I hold a high view of Scripture, and this writing on a resurrection Christology is built on the biblical documents themselves. There is no other source for an understanding of the Resurrection than the Scripture and the Biblicism of this work takes the scripture's accounts as the highest authority. Even though the meaning of our future resurrection is affirmed without our knowing the form in which our resurrected person will come into expression, the message of Scripture is that we will not be disembodied spirits, but we will be like Him, recreated to be actual expressions of the personalities that we are. Remember, Moses and Elijah came and talked with Jesus on the "Mount of Transfiguration" as recognizable persons. Peter recognized them as such, not as mere spirits. Jesus affirmed resurrected personhood in possibly His most remarkable comment on the resurrection, "God is not the God of the dead but of the living" (Luke 20:38).

Again, for me to affirm the Resurrection as the extension and validation of the ministry and death of Jesus of Nazareth means that discipleship is not only to obey the teachings of the man, Jesus, but is solidarity with the risen Jesus by walking with Him in life now. What a fantastic claim. And we do this by walking in the Word and in the Spirit. Discipleship engages the power of grace and truth, for God has come to us in love and truth, joining covenant with us.

Since no one witnessed the Resurrection and it is not verifiable in a scientific fashion, numerous theologians speak more of the meanings of the Resurrection than of its factualness. But in objective study of the New Testament, it becomes clear that the documents speak of the risen Christ and His appearances to His followers in the same factual relation to history as they speak of any other event in the life of Jesus. This is to say that, while we do not have ways of discussing or of pursuing a scientific analysis of the Resurrection itself, we do have actual claims of the disciples having met the risen Christ, of their speaking with Him and eating with Him. They affirmed one another's claim to have seen the risen Christ in a similar way as they describe having spent time with Jesus of Nazareth before the Crucifixion. That they made these claims and lived and died by them is without question historical fact, both as witness and as faith.

Recently in public media, there has been extensive discussion as to whether we actually had men walking on the moon or whether this has been fabricated. All we have are the records and words of witnesses! This is similar with the Resurrection and we have the accounts!

Resurrection is itself the major miracle; but it is a miracle tied to the creative work of God. The miracles in Jesus' ministry were basically extensions of Creation, of His work as Creator in which He is Lord of Creation. They were not simply "wonders" or deeds of magic. This miracle of His Resurrection was expressed in the created order. It was attested by the actual appearances of the risen Jesus. Yoder writes, "Most of the appearances reported in 1 Corinthians 15 were public. Therefore, the absence of any ancient documentation of evidence that would count against it, such as anyone reporting having found the real body of Jesus in a tomb, or any credible ancient document reporting fraudulent actions on the part of the disciples, is a weight of silence. A leadership team knowing they had fabricated false evidence would hardly have produced the New Testament story" (Yoder, *Preface To Theology*, p. 114).

We should again note that the record or accounts of the appearances of the risen Christ to the disciples are historical accounts in a similar way as any and all of the accounts of His deeds and miracles are historical (Matthew 28; Mark 16; Luke 24; John 20-21; Acts 1:1-11; 1 John 1:1-5). This is an important fact and is primary as the basis for saying that the Resurrection is historical, that it is a historical event, and its attestation is historical. As we look at the Gospels they are not copies of each other, they are not identical—their very diversity giving more credibility. But each of them states the essential truth. John writes, "That which was from the beginning, which we have heard, which we have seen with our eyes, which we have looked at and our hands have touched—this we proclaim concerning the Word of life" (1 John 1:1-2). John's testimony is clearly a witness to the historicity of both the Incarnation and the Resurrection.

While writing these lines, *The Washington Post*, August 14, 1992, carried an article entitled, "Remains Linked to High Priest at Trial of Jesus." It reported "The bones of a 1st century man named Caiaphas have been discovered in an ancient burial cave in Jerusalem, and archaeological evidence indicates they may be remains of the high priest who handed Jesus over to the Roman governor Pontius Pilate for execution. The age of the bones, the elaborate ossuary in which they were found and inscriptions with the name Caiaphas on the side of the casket-like box point to the man described in the Gospels, although Israeli archaeologists who found the remains said they cannot be positive." For us, to find the bones of Caiaphas is understandable, but never the bones of Jesus, for the tomb was empty—He is alive!

As an evangelist for nearly fifty years, much of my work has been in interchurch preaching missions that have been very ecumenical, at times including Catholic and Protestant congregations. From these meetings I am known as a 'discipler.' My message in evangelism has been a call for persons to identify with Christ as His disciples. This is a call to covenant, but it is a covenant in grace. The exposure of our rebellion against God is evident at the Cross, and it was God who met us in the Cross. In raising Jesus from the dead, God verified the Cross as a victory of love. And now, with the victory of the risen Christ, God has uniquely come to us again in His Spirit. God accepts us in grace. In Christ, God forgives us in grace, and in the Spirit of Christ, we are empowered to walk with Him in grace.

For fourteen years in Washington, D.C., in planting a church and being pastor for the congregation on Capitol Hill, I have tested this truth and seen the power of the Resurrection at work in a cross-cultural, interracial, inner city and multi-denominational setting. It has been exciting to see the way in which the Spirit of the risen Christ transforms lives and how He can create a very vibrant congregation out of people of great diversity.

In celebrating the Resurrection of our Lord, we take our place in His victorious kingdom. We live now in His victory, in His fellowship, in His power, in His mission, and in His ultimate purpose. God has predestined that our lives are to be "conformed to the image of His Son" (Romans 8:29). We are being shaped by the sovereign Lord Jesus Christ and not by some lesser lord. His lordship means that as our Savior He is our liberator, for He is saving us every day from being what we would be without Him. As head of the church, He calls each of us to participate in fellowship with others who walk with the risen Christ. And when we gather, He is there in our midst. Jesus said, "Lo I am with you always, even to the end of the age" (Matthew 28:20). Let us look now at His continuing presence—He is always "there for us."

2

God's Presence in the Sovereign Spirit

"Now I am going to Him who sent me, yet none of you even asks me, 'where are you going?' Because I have said these things, you are filled with grief. But I tell you the truth: It is for your good that I am going away. Unless I go away, the Counselor will not come to you; but if I go I will send Him to you. When he comes, he will prove the world wrong about sin and righteousness and judgment: about sin, because men do not believe in me; about righteousness, because I am going to the Father, where you can see me no longer; and about judgment, because the prince of this world now stands condemned. I have much more to say to you, more than you can now bear. But when he, the Spirit of truth, comes, he will guide you into all truth. He will not speak on his own; he will speak only what he hears, and he will tell you what is yet to come. He will bring glory to me by taking from what is mine and making it known to you. All that belongs to the Father is mine. That is why I said the Spirit will take from what is mine and make it known to you" (John 16:5-15).

When the risen Jesus led the disciples out to the Mount of Olives, He left them with His blessing. He had given them the simple word that He was going to "the Father." But now He was gone, and how did they know where He was? Further, when He left the disciples, He made them a promise that He would send the Holy Spirit from the Father. He went away and days passed—where was He? The disciples met daily in prayer and discussion, waiting for this promise to be fulfilled. How else were they to know that He was where He said He would be? Was He actually at God's right hand?

And then Pentecost happened! **The coming of the Spirit was their answer. Jesus was just where He said He would be!** He is at the right hand of God! Jesus is both alive and exalted Lord. Peter said, "Being to the right hand of God, exalted, he has now shed forth this which you see and hear" (Acts 2:32-33). This was *their* assurance. And it is *ours*.

A further meaning of Pentecost is the wonderful reality that God is here. He is in the world. He is present with us, in the world now, not removed from it. This is an amazing faith affirmation. **The coming of the Spirit means that God is present.** He is active in the world. We live in a world that tends to ask with every tragedy, "Where is God?" as though God should have intervened and prevented the tragedy. Our answer is that God is here, even suffering with us in the tragedies themselves. When we are honest about the fact that accidents happen, human sinfulness causes suffering, and our universe is not heaven, we can recognize the presence of God with us. God does "allow bad things to happen to good people," and in those things we seek Him.

The coming of the Spirit is the guarantee of the victory of the risen Christ, but we also celebrate the fact that the Spirit of Christ has come to be with us. We are not alone! The sovereign God is present and is at work in the world. And the Spirit is not an add-on to the believer's experience; He is the actual dynamic force that calls us to faith, which transforms us in relationship with God. And this is the Holy Spirit as "person," not merely a divine energy permeating all of life. As believers, "we worship God in the Spirit" (Philippians 3:3). God is not absent—He is here. This is our faith stance, recognition of His sovereign presence at work in a way that is true to His own person and character.

God created us in freedom to graciously share himself with us. His purpose has always been to be present with us. And His being with us is to overcome our perversions of sin, to enable us to walk in victorious freedom. From the beginning, in the Garden of Eden, God walked with our first parents in the cool of the evening, enjoying fellowship with them, until separated by their self-centered action (Genesis 3:8). In the history of Israel, He was present among the people and led them by the "Shekinah" cloud of glory. This was the glory of His presence, by which God also protected them and guided them (Exodus 14:19-20, 40:34-38). There is a wonderful account of the presence of God seen in a cloud by day and a radiant light over the tabernacle at night, the comfort and the searching of His presence, but He was also the One to go before and guide them in life. The passage tells us that when the glory lifted and moved the people followed, and as long as it stayed at rest they stayed in camp (Numbers 9:15-23). To practice God's presence, means that we live by the leading and will of God.

In numerous passages we are told that God gave to individuals the special gift of His Spirit for the work of His kingdom: in art, in music, and in prophetic utterance. On one such occasion, when God gave the elected elders His Spirit, two of them were down in the camp and they began to prophecy. When the others present requested that they should be forbidden to prophecy, Moses said, "Would that all God's people were prophets." Joel, a much later prophet, predicted that this experience would come to pass, and Peter quoted Joel at Pentecost regarding the last days that, "God says, 'I will pour out my Spirit on all people. Your sons and daughters will prophesy, your young men will see visions, and your old men will dream dreams. Even on my servants, both men and women, I will pour out my Spirit in those days and they will prophesy'" (Acts 2:17-18).

In the promise of His coming we read, "You shall call his name Immanuel, which is, God with us" (Matthew 1:23). And again, "The Word was made flesh and dwelled among us" (John 1:14). His life in humanness expressed the character that we are to live through the Spirit. Jesus as the Son of God was able to say, "If you have seen me, you have seen the Father" (John 14:9). As He lived and taught, He expressed in His person the will and work of God.

Now we come to the wonderful promise, that after His Resurrection and Ascension He would send us an advocate, the Holy Spirit, who would be with us and in us (John 14:16-17). The coming of the Spirit on Pentecost was the fulfillment of this promise (Acts 2:1-4). The wonderful thing is that Christ is present now with the believers; that the church is the dwelling of God by the Spirit (1 Corinthians 3:16-17; Ephesians 2:20-22). The individual believer becomes the temple of the Spirit (1 Corinthians 6:19-20) and as such is baptized by one Sprit into the body of Christ (1 Corinthians 12:13). And finally, the goal of our glory is to be present with God in His glory (Revelation 21:1-7)—to dwell in the eternal city where God is the center and glory. His Resurrection is the basis for this reality and the assurance of its fulfillment.

When one sees God's purpose as being with His people, then the presence of the Spirit of God is a fulfillment of God's purpose. The gift of the Spirit, the assurance that Jesus as the One who baptizes with the Spirit is at God's right hand, is essential to the salvation experience. His presence is not an appendage to the salvation experience—it is the heart. We are saved in being reconciled to God by His Son and reconciled means to be in solidarity with Him as confirmed by the presence of the Holy Spirit. To be a participant in authentic salvation is to know the presence and to live in the freedom and the fellowship of the Spirit. Paul writes, "Anyone who does not have the Spirit of Christ does not belong to Him" (Romans 8:9). And again, "For all who are led by the Spirit of God are children of God" (Romans 8:14).

Amazing as it is, we can practice the presence of God. We do not live in the absence of Christ for although He is at God's right hand He is present with us in the Holy Spirit (1 John 3:24). Nor can we live a life of discipleship by our own ability, for discipleship is not simply a standard of living—it is a relationship with the risen Lord. It is impossible to think about walking with the Lord apart from opening our lives to His presence. And His presence is mediated by the Holy Spirit whom Jesus promised and gives to us.

The Jesus who speaks in the text quoted from John 16 at the beginning of this chapter, is the One of whom the same scripture says, "The Word became flesh and dwelled among us." In His incarnation among humanity, it follows that, as long as Jesus was here, we would localize God in Jesus of Nazareth. But Jesus said to His disciples that it was necessary for Him to go to the Father so that the Spirit would come and the presence of God would be universal. This statement made clear that after the resurrection the Spirit would be the universal presence of God among His people. This is a special aspect of the human "problem" of understanding the Trinity; we are a people in "the Name of the Father, Son, and the Holy Spirit."

The resurrection power released in us by the Spirit follows upon our dying with Christ to the former self-centered life (Romans 6:1-6). In fact, there is no resurrection unless there is first death. As we die to our self-centeredness, a break with the old life as definite as death, we are then joined with Christ in His Resurrection power. This transformation is an emptying of self and an infilling with the Spirit. Jesus promised the Spirit as a presence and power that would conform us to His image; for "he shall glorify me," Jesus said. We now have a God-centered life, the birth of a new reality that is transforming in grace.

The coming of the Holy Spirit in a unique and personal way at Pentecost was/is the fulfillment of Jesus' promise to be present with us. God's presence in the world is now primarily in the person of the Holy Spirit, confirming God's self-disclosure in the scriptures and affirming the work of Christ as reconciliation. Prior to the completed work of the Cross and Resurrection as our reconciliation with the Father, the work of the Spirit was limited to preparatory stages. In the Old Testament era, the Holy Spirit came upon select people in which the Spirit made real the presence of God. Following Christ's victory in the Cross and the Resurrection, the Spirit is free to actualize the presence of God in the lives of all who believe. Now the Spirit's engagements are the confirmation of Christ's forgiving, reconciling work.

Jesus said, "It is necessary for you that I go away, if I go not away the Comforter will not come, but if I depart I will send Him unto you," (John 16:7-14). As noted, when Jesus was here God was localized in Jesus, but after His Resurrection and Ascension, Jesus Christ is universalized. This means that God is expressed both as the concrete and now the universal in Jesus Christ. However, the universality of Christ is the universality of the Spirit. This is the mystery of God who as Jesus said, "is Spirit" (John 4:24). As seen in another statement by John, Christ abides in our hearts by the Holy Spirit (1 John 3:23). The risen Lord is among us as God is among us, for God is here in the Holy Spirit. "Our Father" is in heaven. Our Redeemer is at God's right hand, in heaven. Our comforter, our companion— God is with us. Mysterious as it is, He is the presence of God the Father. God is Spirit, and the risen Christ may be thought of as Spirit-Man, for He is with us by the Holy Spirit, and we have the mystery of a Trinitarian presence. The Spirit is God the sanctifier, the God who lays claim to us and who sets us totally apart for God.

The uniqueness of this confirmation is the promise of Christ to baptize with the Spirit each person who accepts Him as Lord. In this gift of presence the individual believer becomes the "temple of the Holy Spirit" (1 Corinthians 6:19-20). By the Spirit's indwelling, the disciple of Christ is empowered to live in the will of Christ. The Baptism with the Spirit is a Baptism we receive from our sovereign Lord Jesus, for He is the Baptizer. This Baptism is the gift of the Spirit's presence. In consequence, this very gift of the Spirit's presence initiates or baptizes us into the body of Christ (1 Corinthians 12:13).

In this relationship, we become a part of all who also know the indwelling of the Spirit. The church, rather than being an institution, is actually a community of the Spirit. Christ creates this one body, this fellowship or community of the Spirit, as the expression of His presence and work in the world. As we think of a resurrection Christology—our beliefs about Christ—we must recognize that Christ is now head of the church. Yet He is known in an intimate way through this gift of the Spirit. Without recognition of the Spirit as a gift from our risen Lord, we have only a partial, truncated faith-experience. He is not absent, He is not a Lord far removed from us, and He is the Lord who has moved into our lives, mediating the reality of God, present as the Spirit.

The risen Lord who lays claim to us and unites us with Himself is thereby creating His church. This church is called the body of Christ. As the body makes a personality visible, so the church as the body of Christ makes Jesus visible to the social order. This is a high calling for the church! We should recognize, in interpreting the text, it is through us who believe that the Spirit convicts the world of its sin of unbelief, of its unrighteousness or broken relationship with God, and of its defeat by the demonic (John 16:8-11). Our freedom in Christ is evidence that the victory of Christ is genuine.

To highlight this text from John, there are three things that Jesus emphasized as the Spirit's action in confronting the world, and they happen through our participation. By His coming, the Spirit will do these things primarily through Christ's disciples. He convinces the world of sin and does so by our expressions of belief in Christ amidst the world's unbelief. He convinces the world of the reality of righteousness, in that since Jesus has gone to the Father, He expresses in us the meaning of the righteousness of God. He convinces the world of judgment, "for the prince of this world is judged," showing in our victorious living that the Evil One has no power over our lives! It is by our victory in the Spirit that He demonstrates that the Devil is already defeated. The Spirit glorifies Christ in us who believe and through us as we walk with Him. Through us as believers Christ is made visible to the world.

In the verses that follow, Jesus speaks of three things that the Spirit will do for us as our resource of grace in the community of faith. He will guide us into the truth, that is, the Spirit will give us insight and spiritual intuition. John writes in his epistle, "You have an anointing of the Holy One and you all know spiritual things" (1 John 2:20). Paul writes to the Corinthians, "No one knows the thoughts of God except the Spirit of God, not in words taught us by human wisdom but in words taught by the Spirit, expressing spiritual truths in spiritual words. The man without the Spirit does not accept the things that come from the Spirit of God for they are foolishness to Him, and he cannot understand them, because they are spiritually discerned" (1 Corinthians 2:12-14). By the Spirit's illumination we are enabled to grasp the spirit of Scripture, to catch its basic meaning. Its inerrancy is not in the words, which may vary from translation to translation, but is rather in an inerrancy of meaning.

The Spirit will not speak on His own. The Spirit will not speak independently from what God has declared in His mighty acts and words in history and which God as Son has declared in His life and ministry. Jesus said, "He will take from what is mine and make it known to you" (John 16:14). This is the same Holy Spirit who acted in the inspiration of Scripture so that the Word written is a Word that is God-breathed, inspired, and infallible in its meaning (2 Timothy 3:16). Again Peter declares of the Scriptures, "Holy men of God spoke as they were carried along by the Holy Ghost" (2 Peter 1:21). This "sure word of prophecy" is a word that is totally trustworthy and its authoritative meaning is made clear by the insights given by the Holy Spirit. We study its words carefully including the original languages to find the meaning of the passage. As we do this, it must be in openness to the Spirit's guidance and to the community of faith in which we exercise a "community hermeneutic" as our discernment in the Spirit. I do not say "corporate hermeneutic" but "community hermeneutic" (interpretation) for we do not necessarily do our interpreting as a group, but we do interpret in relation to the thought of the believing community, whether it be in personal interchange or in our reading and use of sources from others who walk with Christ.

Jesus said, "He will glorify me by taking from what is mine and making it known to you. All that belongs to the Father is mine" (John 16:14-15). What a fantastic claim in terms of the expressions of the three-in-one God! This is the wonderful harmony of the One Divine "Community of Love" expressed in the unexplainable term of Trinity. Paul writes, "There is one body and one Spirit—just as you were called—one Lord, one faith, one baptism; one God and Father of all, who is over all and through all and in all" (Ephesians 4:4-6).

Jesus' words, "He will glorify me," identifies the Spirit's work as an implicit call for us to walk in the Spirit; the character of this walk is to glorify Christ. This is more than a religious claim, for it is a life that is lived in a full and personal identification with Jesus Christ, in walk and word, in praise and prayer, in spirit and fellowship. He is among us and within us; He is known personally and individually but is more fully known as we share in the dynamic of the community He creates. In the larger community the full richness of His gifts are expressed. The Spirit is the enabling presence evidenced in the creative work of His grace in our lives.

It is by walking in the Spirit—that is, acknowledging Him rather than trusting our own abilities—that we have the power to live the new life. It is by the Spirit that we are enabled to live out the new liberating ethic of love. This is our victory. The sovereign Spirit actualizes a new freedom in the believer's life, a freedom to love. More than a behavioral code, this means, as we have noted previously, that we relate ethics to our belonging to Christ in the same way that we relate salvation to belonging to Christ. Again, to say it another way, we are saved by our relation to Jesus and we "behave," or live out, our relation to Jesus!

Paul's benediction extending to us the "communion of the Holy Spirit" is a wonderful expression of the privilege of interchange between the Spirit and us. It corresponds to Jesus' words that He would send us the Comforter (John 14:26-27), the Counselor. These very titles suggest communion, interchange, and fellowship. Further, in Paul's letter to the Romans, he speaks of the Spirit in us and as making intercession for us (Romans 8:26-27). Again he speaks of what John Calvin called the "inner witness" in the words, "The Spirit Himself testifies with our spirit that we are God's children" (Romans 8:16). And, of this communion, Jude teaches us to engage the privilege of "praying in the Holy Spirit" (Jude v. 20). We should take seriously the sovereign presence of the Spirit and carry on prayer conversation with the Spirit over the Word.

As to our life in the Spirit, beyond the fact that it is the Spirit's initiative in calling us to repentance and faith and to a born-again life in grace, there are relational aspects that need to be given their full meaning. We have recognized first the Baptism with the Spirit; a gift of the presence of the Spirit bestowed by Jesus, for Jesus is the One who does the baptizing. Receiving the Spirit should be realized in our experience of salvation and the new birth, but this Baptism with the Spirit even though simultaneous is not synonymous with the new birth. The new birth is the recreating of my spirit in a living fellowship with God, while this inner baptism is the gift of God's Spirit to be present in my life.

My sixteenth century forbearers, the Anabaptists, believed in both the inner baptism and the outer baptism. The "inner" being the Baptism with the Spirit in its liberating and transforming power, while the "outer" is water baptism. This is the sign of covenant that is an expression of identification with Christ, but not by itself transforming. The inner baptism means that we do not only rejoice in being made alive to God, but we celebrate the actual presence of God. This presence of the Spirit is revealed as a comforting, counseling, illuminating, guiding, enabling, or transforming force in the believer's life. God is here within us, present by His Spirit.

There is further a security provided by this "sealing with the Holy Spirit." It effectively keeps us from evil (1 John 5:18), and His presence is our security from the evil one. Paul writes of our being sealed with the Holy Spirit of promise (Ephesians 1:13). His presence is the seal, that is, the sign that we are God's possession. The evil one cannot tamper with us without answering to God. His presence is our protection.

The term used for our continuing experience is the "filling with the Spirit." This is contingent upon our being yielded and willing, for we are commanded to be continually filled (Ephesians 5:18, present imperative tense in the Greek verb meaning something that is commanded and is to be continuous). This filling creates the joy and radiance, the victory and vitality, the spirit and obedience for the person who walks in the Light.

To be filled with the Spirit—filled with this Other—means that we are to be emptied of our selfishness and be open to His presence. If you have a glass filled with water, to fill the glass with milk you must empty the water. Just so we must be emptied of our self-centeredness if we are to be filled with the Spirit in Christ-centeredness.

We also share the fellowship of the Spirit—a personal association with Him but especially in our participation with other believers as members in the body of Christ. The church is a community of the Spirit, and it is the Spirit's presence that enables our communion, our prayers, and our worship to be centered on the reality of God. But there is a fellowship between us, as individual persons, and God. God is mediated to us in the spirit dimension of our lives and this is experienced in the reality of His Presence. This fellowship is the transforming reality of covenant relationship with God.

We are especially enriched by the illumination of the Spirit, the anointing which gives us insight into the Scripture and its revealed truth. This includes the discernment to know when truths are consistent with God's Truth (1 John 2:27). The very Spirit who inspired the Scripture is present to guide us in the interpretation of Scripture. Spiritual things are discerned in the Spirit (1 Corinthians 2). This gift enables us to understand and apply the truth of Scripture in context with our particular culture. As we pray over the scripture we can hear His confirmation of truth.

As we speak of a community hermeneutic, it is the discernment of sincere Christian believers that helps us to distinguish between our spirit and the insights of the Holy Spirit. It is in exercising this interpretive role that we serve and enrich one another. It is also a function in accountability to the Word itself.

We are graced with the Fruit of the Spirit, with all of the meanings that begin in His love. Jesus said, "If anyone thirst let Him come to me and drink and out of His inner being will flow rivers of living water." This is a wonderful reference to the life of the Spirit providing fruitfulness (John 7:37). As I studied the list of Spirit fruit in Galatians 5:22, recognizing the primacy of love, it struck me that I could interpret each of the words which follow as expressions of love. By this I am saying that joy is the celebration of love, peace is the practice of love, patience is the preservation of love, kindness is the expression of love, goodness is the action of love, faithfulness is the loyalty of love, gentleness is the attitude of love, and self-control is the restraint of love! The fruit of the Spirit is love. And love covers over, that is to say, prevents a multitude of sins!

Fruit grows on the branches but it draws its sustenance from the vine. Jesus is the Vine, and we are the branches. It is our relationship with Him that enables us to bear fruit for the kingdom. We should not shrink from His pruning away the deadness that tends to beset our lives, for in doing so He enables new growth. In trimming my actual grape vines in our back yard, I have discovered that the fruit always appears on the new growth!

We are empowered by the Spirit with gifts that will enrich both the personal life and also the life of the congregation of believers. I see no reason from Scripture to say that these gifts were limited to any one time but may be given "according to His will" at any time and to any people (Hebrews 2:4). Paul's lengthy treatment of this matter, his effort to correct persons from being more interested in the gifts than in the Giver, is expressed clearly and emphatically in 1 Corinthians 12-14. The presentation of His gifts begins with "wisdom" (1 Corinthians 12:8), and since He is the sovereign Giver, we respect His selection and endowment for we, too, need to begin with His wisdom. While some would elevate the spiritual gift of speaking in tongues higher than Paul does, we should note that the Spirit also grants a special prophetic role to persons who are thereby enabled to help others in sharing God's message with discernment and interpreting God's calling to discipleship.

As Paul concludes chapter twelve, his words are ambiguous in saying either that the Corinthians were being commanded "to covet earnestly the better gifts" or that they were being described as "always coveting" the best gifts (1 Corinthians 12:31). There is a problem left to us in the interpretation of this phrase because the verb as expressed in the Greek language is identical in both the imperative and the indicative mood. The ambiguity is on the matter of the meaning of the verb. If it is the "imperative" we are being commanded to seek the better gifts. If so, in my opinion, this would not mean a hierarchy of gifts but rather a seeking of the better gift for equipping in the role in which we are called to serve. But if it is the "indicative" mood, then it is descriptive of a condition among the people of God that needs correction. If it is this, Paul is characterizing the behavior of the Corinthian church, saying, "You Corinthians are always seeking the better gifts," i.e., the more spectacular gifts, vying for status. This latter interpretation may well be the contextual choice, for he continues by saying, "But I show you a more excellent way," the way of love in practice. This latter interpretation may emphasize the uniqueness of this passage in context, for placed between these two chapters on gifts, he places one of the most beautiful presentations on love to be found in any literature (1 Corinthians 13).

Above all, the Spirit transforms us to be "conformed to the image of God's Son" (Romans 8:29). This is the purpose and goal of the Spirit's work in our lives. Redemption is confirmed in our belonging to God. Our justification is assured in the grace of Christ. Through His reconciliation, we are made holy in now belonging wholly to God. Paul adds, we are glorified by the Shekinah (glow) of the Spirit's presence (Romans 8:30). It is by His power that we are enabled to know the victory of freedom from the dominance of sin.

Again he writes: "But you are not in the flesh; you are in the Spirit, since the Spirit of God dwells in you. Anyone who does not have the Spirit of Christ does not belong to him. But if Christ is in you, though the body is dead because of sin, the Spirit is life because of righteousness. If the Spirit of him who RAISED JESUS FROM THE DEAD dwells in you, he who raised Christ from the dead will give life to your mortal bodies also through his Spirit that dwells in you. So then, brothers and sisters, we are debtors, not to the flesh, to live according to the flesh—for if you live according to the flesh, you will die; but if by the Spirit you put to death the deeds of the body, you will live. For all who are led by the Spirit of God are children of God. For you did not receive a spirit of slavery to fall back into fear, but you have received a spirit of adoption. When we cry, 'Abba! Father!' It is that very Spirit bearing witness with our spirit that we are children of God, and if children, then heirs, heirs of God and joint heirs with Christ—if, in fact, we suffer with him so that we may also be glorified with him" (Romans 8:9-17).

Since the Reformation, the Protestant Church has had a strong and wonderful emphasis on justification by faith and on the universal priesthood of the believer. But, with these strengths, Protestants have also carried with them the danger of excessive individualism. We have not taken seriously enough the transforming work of the Spirit expressed in the creation of a new people—a new community. We need to recognize the act of God in reconciling grace and that our justification by faith is based on His act of reconciliation (Romans 5:9-11), (see my book, *The Robe of God*). In this reconciliation, we share a oneness with God and with one another mediated by our Lord Jesus Christ. This dynamic of community frees or liberates us from an individualism that limits mutuality in the body of Christ.

God is at work through the Spirit building His kingdom in the world. The mission that Christ made clear continues. It is extended through us who have been given the message and the ministry of reconciliation (2 Corinthians 5:18-20). But this is not a work that we own or that we fulfill in ourselves, it is the work of the Spirit and we are His instruments. Paul writes, "We have this treasure in earthen vessels that the excellence of the power may be of God and not of us" (2 Corinthians 4:7). The Spirit is God's presence in the world, and we are privileged to share in his work. It is our responsibility to seek together an understanding of the will of God, to look in the Word and in life for the way in which the Spirit is at work, and participate with Him. Let us look now at the mission of the Spirit, in and through us, making faith in Christ a possibility for others.

3

Making Faith an Option

"And he died for all, so that those who live might live no longer for them-
selves, but for him who died AND WAS RAISED FOR THEM. From
now on, therefore, we regard no one from a human point of view; even though
we once knew Christ from a human point of view, we know him no longer
in that way. So if anyone is in Christ, there is a new creation: everything old
has passed away; see, everything has become new! All this is from God, who
reconciled us to himself through Christ, and has given us the extended MIN-
ISTRY OF RECONCILIATION; that is, in Christ God was reconciling
the world to himself, not counting their trespasses against them, and entrust-
ing the message of reconciliation to us. So we are ambassadors for Christ,
since God is making his appeal through us; we entreat you on behalf of
Christ, be reconciled to God. For our sake he made him to be sin who knew
no sin, so that in him we might become the righteousness of God"
(2 Corinthians 5:15-21).

Following His Resurrection, as Christ met with the disciples
regularly during a 40-day period, He gave the disciples a special
mission. His announcement was two-fold, "You will receive the
power of the Holy Spirit coming upon you...and you will be my

witnesses" (Acts 1:8). Beyond Pentecost is the further commission to be His witnesses. Both the promise of the Spirit and the commission extends to us; we are ambassadors for the risen Christ. We share His Resurrection fellowship and we become witnesses of this reality.

Thomas said he could not believe unless he saw the marks in the hands of the risen Christ. And we, too, look for the marks of the crucified One. And we see those marks in every expression of His transforming grace, in lives that His hands have touched. And we have seen those marks in many countries and cultures of the world where meeting the risen Lord is marked by His transforming power.

Teaching at Union Biblical Seminary, Pune, India, in the fall of 2002, I was gripped by the remarkable testimony of a member of my class. As a young lad (I will call him Kumar), one of several sons in the home of a wealthy Muslim businessman had a dream or vision. One night he heard Jesus say to him, "Come unto me, all ye that labor and are heavy laden, and I will give you rest." He had never heard those words, had never read a Bible. The next morning he told his father, and in turn, his father told Him to just forget it—to put it out of his mind.

But he remembered, and one day his vehicle stopped in front of a church and he went in to use the telephone. He met the pastor, and as they chatted, he told the pastor this story. Without a word, the pastor reached over and picked up a Bible, opened to Matthew 11, and pointed to the last two verses. Kumar read, "Come unto me all ye that labor and are heavy laden and I will give you rest." He was dumbstruck. As a result, he became a believer and was baptized but didn't tell his father. One day his father said, "Kumar, what is so different about you? You have changed, and you don't run with the old crowd." Kumar said, "I've become a Christian and I've been baptized."

His Muslim father said in some heat, "Out, get out, and don't come back until you come back a Muslim." Kumar went to his room to pack up, and his father came to the door, "What are you doing?" Kumar replied, "I'm packing up. You told me to leave." His father said sharply, "You leave, nothing else goes with you, it stays here." Kumar left a family and a wealthy home, and did so with only the shirt on his back.

He went to the pastor who felt it wise to send Kumar away to avoid danger, and he sent Him to Calcutta to work at an orphanage. The persons in charge had question whether a young man from a high-level family and Muslim background could be a sincere believer, and so they put him to the lowest task conceivable—cleaning the toilets, and you must realize that the Indian toilet is basically a hole over which you stand or squat. They said, "If he is not sincere he won't stick." But he stuck it out. Today he is a senior at the seminary, married to an American woman, and they are planning to go into mission work among their Muslim friends. In his story I have seen the marks of the nails.

The risen Christ has given us a commission, to be His witnesses in all societies. This is not manipulation salesmanship but a witness of knowing and walking with Jesus. Evangelism is making faith in Christ an option, a possibility, for other persons. As we share our remarkable privilege and joy of walking with Jesus in life, this solidarity with Him becomes a witness of His transforming grace. In this walk of discipleship, an evangelistic witness issues from the very freedom of spirit in one's life. It is not an appendage or an activity in itself but is a way of compassionate living. **Evangelism is anything and everything that makes faith in Christ a possibility for persons.** It involves the total of one's life as a presence for Christ and His kingdom.

Our approach to others should be made in the way in which we would like others to approach us. It is an approach that is above all in the spirit of Jesus. While given in freedom, it must never violate the other's freedom. Further, it is the uniqueness of

Jesus Christ, who He is and what He does for us that makes us evangelists. Unfortunately, many people, reluctant to be involved in evangelism, are conditioned by some of the patterns of religious huckstering prevalent in our time. Or we react to some psychological conditioning arising from some unfortunate approach of religious manipulation. But there are other models, including that of Christ as well as His apostles. We need to refine the role of evangelism and to see that it is pursued with integrity, respect, and passion.

When Paul lists gifts that the risen Christ has given, they include apostles, prophets, evangelists, pastors, and teachers. We seem to minimize the role of the evangelist. We could just as critically point out the authoritarian and the manipulative ways in which persons have served as prophetic leaders, as pastors, and as teachers. In any role, we are vulnerable to human pride and ego patterns, and each area of service calls for the sanctifying work of the Spirit. We should pray for the Lord of the church to give those gifts needed, especially the gift of evangelism.

There are theologians within the church who reveal a bias against evangelism in their comments, but if you read carefully, it becomes evident that their theology is more a philosophy than a witness. They do not have the "good news" of Christ to offer persons as a basis of faith for engagement with God's transforming grace. But what a refreshing voice in the late Lesslie Newbigin who—as a missionary statesman, a global evangelist, and a keen theologian—has left us with the very significant work, *The Gospel in a Pluralist Society*. I shall long remember his uncompromising statement of the Gospel in one of the meetings we shared, affirming of the Gospel, "The Resurrection fits no other world view!"

William Temple, who became the Archbishop of Canterbury, said at the Jerusalem meeting of the International Missionary Council in 1928, "The message of the church to the world is, and must always remain, the Gospel of Jesus Christ—we cannot

live without Christ and we cannot bear to think of (others) living without Him."

We believe that the disclosure of God to humanity came into
its full focus in Jesus Christ. Therefore, we proclaim Christ not
to put down other religions but to present in Christ the answer
from God to the religious quest of others. To the Jews, we present Jesus as the full expression of all to which their religion was
calling them. To the Greeks, or Gentiles, we present Jesus as the
answer to all the philosophical questions about the "first Cause"
or the "Unmoved Mover" of their religious quest. In spite of
current modern thought that asks of truth systems how any one
can claim to be the one truth, we are not dealing primarily with
thought systems but with the question of relationship with God
and the claim that this one reality, reconciliation with God, is the
central and exclusive issue.

In the early sixties I had the privilege of hearing both Dr.
Karl Barth and Dr. D. T. Niles at Union Theological Seminary,
Richmond, Virginia. Dr. Barth spoke of the uniqueness of
God's self-disclosure and our need to hear the three-in-one God
in Christ as the Word. D. T. Niles spoke to the uniqueness of the
Gospel in relation to other world religions. In answer to the
question of whether people of other religions could be saved
through their religion without knowing Christ, he said, "If they
are saved it is because of what Christ has done for us all." He
urged us to rethink our mission strategy, to remove the control
patterns of the Western missionary, and to mix with the peoples
among whom we share the gospel on a basis of equity and social
respect. His critique of the period of mission expansion, now
seen as colonialism, was made by an illustration. "In the past,"
he said, "missions has been like a man planting a tree, building
a fence around the tree to protect it, and then spending all of the
time keeping up the fence." People of all religions should know
what God has expressed in Jesus. This word of grace is far more
than the confrontation of competing religions.

It is good news to know a sovereign God who has come to us, who has made himself known to us, who has acted to reconcile us and who creates a new people in the world. This is the word of grace that we share. What makes us evangelists is the fact that we are witnesses of the reality of Christ who by His very person-power calls people to God. He is the Reconciler, the One who brings us into the family of God. The word of Christ is the greatest witness we have to offer! And this sharing can be done with respect and in a witness dialogue, but always with the awareness that the uniqueness of Christ and the work of the Spirit will be calling or inviting the other person in the dialogue to go beyond our words and open their life to God.

By way of definition, evangelism is the sharing of the good news of God's grace expressed in Jesus Christ. Again, evangelism is making faith in Christ a possibility for people. It is not merely a proselytizing of persons from one religion to another, but it is the calling of persons to respond to the God of whom religion can only remind us. It is helping people to find His covenant of love in which we are made new persons. It is bringing into a person's life the dimensions of faith, assurance, and freedom found in moving beyond religious precepts into relationship. Evangelism is not simply confronting persons with doctrine, or with a philosophy of truth to which we ask them to subscribe, but it is calling persons to open themselves to God in a personal act of faith. It is to help a person to accept Jesus in all that He is and will be to us.

To define evangelism as everything that makes faith in Christ possible for all people means we combine living in service roles along with verbal expressions in sharing the message. The evangelistic and the social expressions of the life of the disciple are to be held together, not separated, for both are to be a witness for Christ. In fact, it is the social dimension that prepares the way for others to hear our verbal witness as authenticated by our expressions of love. Our deeds of love authenticate our words, and our words interpret our deeds.

In 1987 Esther and I were teaching at Union Biblical Seminary, Puna, India. On a weekend we flew to Madras to serve at the St. George Cathedral with Bishop Azariah. Following the morning service, as we walked across the grounds, we observed a group of people on the sidewalk along Cathedral Road. Bishop Azariah pointed to a man standing at the end of the crowd of poor people and lepers, and said, "You must meet that man, standing there with the young boy, his son. But first I must tell you about him." He then related to me how this man was a shoe cobbler who sat everyday on the sidewalk in the hot sun repairing shoes and umbrellas, earning perhaps 25 rupees a day, about 75 cents in our currency. Further, one day someone left a baby girl at the cobbler's door, and he and his wife raised the little girl. When she became a teenager, she left and tried unsuccessfully to find her mother. She was pregnant when she returned. The cobbler and his wife took her in again, cared for her, and when she had the baby they took their few rupees and paid her medical costs. They also took her to church and had the baby christened and the mother baptized. Later the man's wife died and the young mother took her baby and left. The shoe cobbler then sent his two older children to boarding school and cared for the younger son, who was blind and helping him at his trade.

Bishop Azariah said, "One day I went to the staff here at the Cathedral and said, 'You see our friend sitting in the hot sun on the sidewalk day after day repairing shoes. Let's take up an offering and give Him money to build a little platform to get up off of the sidewalk, and to build a canopy to keep the sun off his head.' And so we took up an offering, about 300 rupees, and I went across the street and said, 'Friend, your friends here at the Cathedral see you sitting out here day after day in the hot sun on the sidewalk in your work, and we have taken up an offering for you so that you can build a platform up off of the sidewalk and put a canopy over your head to shade you. Here are 300 rupees as a gift.'" Bishop Azariah told us the cobbler's amazing response. The man said, "Thank you, but no thanks. Just as soon as you lift me one foot above the sidewalk my friends will no longer come and sit along side of me and talk." As I listened to the story, my response was that this was a louder sermon than the one I had just preached in the Cathedral!

The church is a fellowship in grace and the only way the church has to exist is to keep reproducing itself by calling new persons—calling each new generation—to Christ. The church is not a religious club, but a fellowship of the redeemed, a community of the reconciled. Actually, the evangelistic aspect of the message of Christ must be heard first in the church by the expressions of nurture and of proclamation so that each new generation may come to put its trust in God through the gospel of Jesus Christ. Evangelism is extended by the sharing of the good news of Jesus with all people, sharing beyond the community of faith. Evangelism is the church, as someone has said, making Christ visible, intelligible, and desirable in society.

It was Erasmus who told the story of Jesus returning to heaven. Michael, the archangel asked, "But Lord, what happens now?" And Jesus replied, "I left eleven men with the responsibility to carry on my work." Michael said, "But Lord, if they fail what then?" Jesus answered, "I have no other plan."

But beyond discussing evangelism as a calling, as a ministry, we must look at the more basic change that the Resurrection brings into focus for the message of the evangel. Jesus himself is now the Gospel. In His ministry, Jesus came announcing the Gospel of the kingdom, the good news of the rule of God, but following His death and Resurrection, Jesus becomes the Good News, He is the King! He is the Gospel, for His death and Resurrection have become the core or heart of the message. He is the one in whom we are reconciled to God. His Resurrection is the unique message that lifts Him above all religions. Just as His Resurrection created faith in the disciples, transformed their lives, and sent them out into the world as "messengers of reconciliation," so our participation in solidarity with and freedom of the resurrected Lord now engages us.

Jesus is now *our* message. The earliest sermons in the book of Acts focus on "this same Jesus" whom God has made both Lord and Christ; or again on "the Name," that "through faith in his Name" we are given eternal life (Acts 2:22-37, 3:11-26). This is not simply a Pauline refocusing of the message as some have claimed. It is the earliest message from the day of Pentecost; it was the message of Peter, of Stephen, of Philip, of the apostles as a group. A totally new community developed around Jesus as Lord (Acts 2:42-47, 4:32-37) and this community gave witness to the Resurrection (Acts 4:33). Christ Jesus is the One in whom we meet the transcendent God who drew close to us and became understandable in Jesus of Nazareth.

As Peter said, "Salvation is found in no one else, for there is no other name under heaven given to men by which we must be saved" (Acts 4:12). That is, salvation is the gift of God. The intent of the quotation is to liberate us from the human search for ways of salvation and to focus us on "The Way" God has provided! God is gracious, and does not leave us lost in our own quest. Some years later Paul wrote to the Corinthians in similar words of this certainty, "For no one can lay any foundation other than the one already laid, which is Jesus Christ" (1 Corinthians 3:11). This was the favorite text of Menno Simons, the 16th century Reformation leader from whom the Mennonite denomination was named. And it aptly expresses the faith and history of Mennonites and other Christians as well.

This word is good news in the midst of the hundreds of religions in the world that reach groping hands toward God, for we have this unique message of grace *in which God reaches to us*. As

John reports, Jesus himself said, "I am the way and the truth and the life. No one comes to the Father except through me" (John 14:6). This is a statement of good news; our search for God in the many and various patterns among religions has been answered, simplified, clarified in the person of Jesus Christ. This Jesus is our Savior and we need no one else! This is the good news of assurance. If we would honestly come to God we must hear Him as God and meet God in the person in whom He comes to us. This is wonderful! We don't have to find God—He has already come to us!

Abraham is not our savior. Moses is not our savior. Buddha is not our savior. And no one since Jesus—Muhammad, Joseph Smith, or any others—supersedes Jesus as the Savior. There are those who make of Jesus Christ less than God's full self-disclosure, and see in Him an expression of God's revelation that may have come in similar forms of revelation to various other peoples. It is said that such revelations were found in persons such as Abraham, Buddha, Muhammad, Joseph Smith, and Sun Myung Moon. But revelation is God's self-disclosure expressed in and of himself in Christ, the One who said, "If you have seen me you have seen the Father."

Today we hear it said that rather than recognizing our limitations and sinfulness, we are to find God within ourselves. This modern stance would actually deify us by having us find God within the human spirit. In John 10:34, Jesus quoted from Psalm 82:6, that God lifted some men to be judges in Israel and designated their role as being gods for Israel and the text clearly states that Jehovah stands among them as judge. This is hardly a passage that suggests the deification of humanity, especially as quoted in a context in which Jesus is presenting himself as the Shepherd and the door to the fold of God! But more seriously, for us to shrink God to human dimensions, so that He may fit our ideas, depersonalizes Him and makes of God simply a universal soul or spirit. With this view God is no longer the One beyond us to whom we answer and to whom we are accountable but only a "god-ness" within us. But the Gospel says that Jesus is beyond us calling us to walk with Him. He alone is our Savior, He is the one Incarnation of God, the one in whom God is fully known, the One in whom God was expressed concretely. I affirm with Karl Barth, "Either Jesus Christ was actually God, or we don't have a full revelation yet."

There are Christians among us whose philosophy of missions would have us not evangelize Jews or Muslims for as is claimed, "They are also children of Abraham." But Abraham is not our savior; he is only an example of faith. Jesus is our Savior, our Redeemer. In no other person do we have a completed work of reconciliation, expressed in the Incarnation, the Cross, the Resurrection, and Ascension. When the early Christians went about sharing the good news, it was not a statement of what they already had in Abraham but was the good news of Jesus *as promised to Abraham*, a patriarch who stands at the beginning of "Heilsgeschichte," (German for salvation history). Salvation history is the movement of God's unfolding plan in history, His saving grace expressed in its culmination in Christ.

Many religions of the world are basically human philosophies. One can better understand Islam if we recognize the Greek philosophy so basic in its development, a philosophy in which the divine is seen as "universal soul" with the result that the Incarnation is "foolishness to the Greek" (1 Corinthians 1:18-25). Jacques Ellul deals extensively with this issue in relation to Islam in his, *The Subversion of Christianity* (chapter 5). He states emphatically, "I believe that in every respect the spirit of Islam is contrary to that of the revelation of God in Jesus Christ. It is (contrary) in the basic fact that the God of Islam cannot be incarnate. This God can be only the sovereign judge who ordains all things as he wills. Another point of antithesis lies in the absolute integration of religious and political law. The expression of God's will inevitably translates itself into law—religious law, inspired by God. Reciprocally, God's will must be translated into legal terms. Islam pushed to an extreme a tendency that is virtual in the Hebrew Bible, but there it is symbolic of the spiritual and is then transcended by Jesus Christ. With Islam we come back to legal formulations as such" (p. 98). But quite often we hear the testimony of seekers who have been confronted by the risen Christ, often in a dream!

Following a discussion of relationship with God, Ellul places the Islamic view of each child being born a Muslim in contrast with the evangelical call for each person to have a personal conversion. He explains, "Now we have to say that this is the very opposite of what may be seen in the Gospels and in Paul. It negates the unique redemptive worth of the death of Jesus Christ" (p. 105). Our Muslim friends must be encouraged to look beyond the exercises of religion in approach to Allah to recognize that "Allah" is the One God who has made and makes himself known in Jesus.

The biblical God opens up freedom for us in His grace and unites us to himself in Christ, the One who has perfect unity with God. The God revealed in Christ is not merely providence, not a deterministic power, but is a personal God. God is the Father of our Lord Jesus Christ, and in Him the God and Father of us all. The call to conversion affirms that God calls and treats all persons alike, inviting each one to respond to Him rather than to trust in their religious heritage or achievements. Furthermore, an invitation to conversion is one of the highest compliments given to us, for it is the affirmation that we can make a responsible choice and say, "yes" to God.

There are many biblical presentations that salvation is by grace through faith rather than through trust in religious engagements. These are frequent in the New Testament and are especially clear in the accounts of the various apostles in their ministry among and to the Jewish communities. This is evident in Paul's work and in his epistles, his letter to the Galatians being very clear on the centrality and finality of redemption in Christ rather than in the Law.

When Paul entered a city, he usually went first to the synagogue as he presented the gospel and taught the "children of Abraham" about Jesus. He built on the meanings of their religious history, showing them the nature of God's self-disclosure, which reached its full expression in Christ. His emphasis on the Incarnation, Death, and Resurrection was central (see Acts 28:23,31). The apostle John is very clear in his message of Christ, especially in his first epistle. Our mission is the same, to share the gospel of God, a gospel of grace that has continued to break into human history from Abraham's dawning of faith to the coming of Jesus, in which the full expression of grace in God's unlimited love is made known for all peoples.

In the epistle of Romans, Paul has an extensive section of three chapters on reconciliation (chapters 9-11), in which he makes clear that salvation is by faith, by the work of Christ, and by God's election in grace. These chapters are a treatment of the place of reconciliation in salvation history. Salvation is not by claims of birth or heredity, nor is it by our works of religious quality but by identification with Christ. Salvation is a great equalizer, for all alike come to God on the basis of God's loving, gracious acceptance.

In Galatians Paul gives us a penetrating treatise on salvation as based on faith in Christ rather than on being children of Abraham or on being persons of the law. He writes, "If you belong to Christ, then you are Abraham's seed and heirs according to the promise" (Galatians 3:29). And again he emphasizes that it is not in being Jew or Gentile, circumcised or uncircumcised, that the issue is decided, but it is by our being made new creatures in Christ (Galatians 6:14-15). The resurrection of Jesus makes it impossible to say anything other than that salvation is provided for all peoples, and only in saying this can we be true to the Scripture.

I have often pointed out in my university classes that if you really want to engage the demanding thing in life and study, become an "avant-garde conservative theologian." To be a liberal is much easier because you can simply project your philosophy and engage its implications. But to be an accomplished conservative theologian is most demanding for it means a mastery of the historical, biblical, and classical interpretations in consistency with the whole. This is essential if we are to be fair to the hearer in our presentation of the Gospel.

I have also frequently said that what makes me an evangelist is not my personality, nor my gifts, but rather my theology. I believe that "If anyone is in Christ that person is a new creation" (2 Corinthians 5:17). The individual as a believer becomes a new creation and becomes part of a new order. This is a message to make each of us an evangelist. It became the central conviction of the Anabaptists, the evangelical heritage from the 16th century for Baptists, Mennonites, and other Free Church groups. In carrying out this conviction, they developed a believer's church, a voluntary fellowship of the reborn, a new community of the redeemed, and a people walking in the resurrection.

While the Protestant groups were tied to the formal pattern of the State Church, with new members being primarily the infants baptized into the church, the Free Church went across the land preaching the Gospel of salvation in Christ to all people. In spite of being mocked as itinerants and hedge-preachers, they carried out their mission of calling persons to Christ, to share in a voluntary decision to commit themselves to solidarity with Christ. In 1525 some of the earliest Anabaptists of the Swiss Brethren actually talked of crossing the ocean to share the Gospel with "the red Jews across the sea," meaning the Native Americans. For their independence from the State Church in calling for a believer's church they were martyred by the thousands. But we must ask where did those thousands come from? They were each won to the faith of Christ by the witness of others to express this new covenant in baptism as believers.

The early leaders of this movement, Conrad Grebel, Felix Mantz, and George Blaurock, were each in their way effective evangelists. Grebel baptized over two hundred in one day on Palm Sunday in the River Sitter at St. Gaul. Felix Mantz, his associate and an effective evangelist, was sentenced to death by drowning, January 5, 1527, with one of the statements condemning him being that his purpose was to evangelize and add members to the movement. This development of a free church, a believer's church, was seen as a threat to the landed State Church. George Blaurock traveled widely in evangelistic missions and then went to take the place of a pastor who was martyred at Gufidan on the Swiss-Italian border and in 1528 was martyred as well. I have visited the castle dungeon where he was chained to a large rock awaiting trial. One cannot help but be impressed with his steadfast faith to endure such an experience.

Leonard Dorfbrunner, an imperial knight from Nuremburg, converted in the spring of 1527. He was commissioned at the Augsburg synod in August 1527, to serve as an evangelist and was martyred in January of 1528 in Austria. Dorfbrunner converted and baptized over three thousand persons in that period of little more than four months of service. What an amazing record of God's work through his short ministry!

Menno Simons was an itinerant evangelist, traveling across the Netherlands and North Germany over a twenty-five year period. We have no way of knowing the number of converts and baptisms he conducted, but one of his colleagues, Leonart Bowens, had a list of some ten thousand persons that he personally had baptized in the Netherlands and North Germany. Menno was hardly less successful. The spread of the movement was primarily by evangelistic teaching and preaching involving men and women in the various ministries of proclamation.

For those in the believer's church, Anabaptists tradition—that is Mennonite/Baptist churches—evangelism is to be seen as an essential aspect of the theology and the life of the church. In fact, the only way in which members come into a believer's church is by personal confession of Jesus Christ. As the late Harold Bender once said to me, as we discussed my evangelistic work and his role as a churchman, "conversion and church are related as cause and effect." The only way in which the believer's church can exist is by the work and spirit of evangelism. But as with many groups, the Mennonite communities of this believer's church movement have tended to become more ethnic and less engaged in evangelistic outreach. The Baptist communities have given evangelism a higher priority, while Mennonites have often given social dimensions more prominence. We need to be more consistent in holding both aspects together.

One sign that a church group has become an ethnic group rather than a dynamic church is when it reproduces itself primarily by the ethnic birth rate. This can happen both among groups that practice infant baptism and among groups, even though they practice believer's baptism, that become more internalized than evangelistic.

Speaking of evangelism as the larger mission of the church, Dr. David Bosch has said, "The church discovers her true nature only as she moves from one human world to another, when she crosses frontiers, whether these are geographical, cultural, ethnic, linguistic, or sociological" (p. 58). It is as we move toward others in the evangelistic ministry, that we actually express the true nature of the Christian message. It is "good news" for all peoples. As Anabaptists, when we unite with Christ in His sufferings, we unite with the suffering of the world with whom He unites. Jesus said of our mission. "As the Father hath sent me, so send I you" (John 20:21).

When the risen Christ was ready to ascend to the Father, according to St. Matthew's gospel, Jesus said to the disciples, "All authority in heaven and on earth has been given to me. Therefore go and make disciples of all nations, baptizing them into the name of the Father and of the Son and of the Holy Spirit, and teaching them to obey everything I have commanded you. And surely I am with you always, to the very end of the age" (Matthew 28:19-20). The imperative is in the phrase, "make disciples of all peoples." This could be expressed as, "While going about in your personal world, your social world, your professional world, your business world, make disciples of all peoples." The scope is, "all peoples," all ethnicities, the creation of a new unified humanity. This awareness and focus is especially relevant in this day which Samuel Huntington of Harvard describes by the new phenomena of relationships in his "Wars of Civilizations." We need a focus which lets us bridge civilizations.

Further, this text makes it evident that evangelism is the mandate of the risen Jesus, not a coercive power struggle of any one group but a gospel equally relevant to all peoples. He expects His followers to spread the good news of God's grace and kingdom throughout the world. It is a trans-cultural mission, trans-racial, trans-national, trans-everything! This is a mission in which we are called to witness to the most radical thing in human thought—Jesus Christ is alive, He is at God's right hand, He has a kingdom in and for this world, and therefore every person should confess Him as Lord (Philippians 2:9-11). The first expression of discipleship among us who declare ourselves as followers of Christ is to take up our Lord's mission. Then, other aspects of discipleship follow alongside for they are quality expressions of how we engage this mission in our daily lives.

According to the opening of the book of the Acts, the risen Christ met with His disciples for a period of forty days, discussing things pertaining to the kingdom of God. In this same period He made them a promise, "You will receive the power of the Holy Spirit coming upon you; and *you will be my witnesses*, in Jerusalem, and in all Judea and Samaria, and to the ends of the earth" (Acts 1:8). And this is the pattern of the book of the Acts—which is really the book of the "acts of the Holy Spirit" through the disciples in their witness of Christ.

As we follow them in Acts, we are confronted with the amazing growth and spread of the church:

♦ In chapter two there were 3000 baptized.

♦ In chapter four the number added was about 5000, including many priests and leaders of the Jews—further, the number not only grew but multiplied.

♦ In chapter seven Stephen, the Hellenist, was calling persons to faith in Christ.

♦ In chapter eight Philip preached in Samaria with many converts, being so successful that Peter and John needed to go to Samaria to confirm the believers as part of the one body of Christ so that their baptism with the Holy Spirit could be confirmed by the Jerusalem representatives.

♦ And, in the last part of chapter eight, Philip is seen with the Ethiopian Eunuch from the staff of Candace, queen of the Ethiopians, leading him to faith and baptism.

♦ In chapter nine Saul of Tarsus was converted to become the apostle Paul, and from here on the story of the Acts primarily follows Paul's ministry to the population centers of the known world, with the concluding phase being his presence in Rome, the center of the world at that time.

While the New Testament account follows Paul north and west, through Asia Minor eventually to Rome, actually the larger growth of the church numerically was more likely to the south, across North Africa. But the book of Acts documents how the church spread all of the way to Rome and beyond, penetrating the cities and centers of civilization of the time, until Paul could say that the gospel had gone into all of the known world (Colossians 1:6).

It takes only a bit of reflection to recognize that most of Paul's prison epistles were written to churches, which he had planted in evangelism. He wrote letters to new Christians, passing on the truth of the gospel. The growth of the early church was extended by their faithful evangelism. This is the mandate of the risen Christ, to carry on His work, to bring the good news of the gospel into all the world. Probably not more than thirty years after Paul we have the letters to the churches of Asia Minor (Revelation chapters two and three), letters the risen Christ asked John and his community to write as a word of judgment, correction, and encouragement.

Several of the most remarkable passages on evangelism are found in Paul's letters to the Corinthians. Paul was an expert at what today is called contextualizing the gospel or putting the good news in terms of the language and concepts of the culture. Paul says that to the Jew he became a Jew, to the weak he became weak: "I have become all things to all men, so that by all possible means I might save some. I do all this for the sake of the gospel, that I may share in its blessings" (1 Corinthians 9:22-23). This calls us to identify with and treat as equal those whom we would reach for Christ.

In another reference Paul refers to our responsibility to not cause anyone to stumble, "Whether Jews, Greeks or the church of God—even as I try to please everybody in every way. For I am not seeking my own good but the good of many, so that they may be saved. Follow my example as I follow the example of Christ" (1Corinthians 10:31-11:1).

In a further passage Paul says, "Since we know what it is to fear the Lord we try to persuade persons" (2 Corinthians 5:11). And again, "For Christ's love compels us. He died for all that those who live should no longer live for themselves but for him who died for them and was raised again" (2 Corinthians 5:14-15). The life of faith is to live for Christ. We are calling people to more than following a code of conduct—but to a fellowship with our risen Lord.

This text is followed by one of the more remarkable theological passages on our unique calling as agents of reconciliation. "All this is from God, who reconciled us to himself through Christ giving us the ministry of reconciliation: that God was reconciling the world to himself in Christ, not counting men's sins against them. And he has committed to us the message of reconciliation. We are therefore Christ's ambassadors, as though God were making his appeal through us. We implore you on Christ's behalf: Be reconciled to God" (2 Corinthians 5:18-20). The use of the plural suggests we all are called to carry on the work of the risen Christ. Dr. Art McPhee calls it "Friendship Evangelism," a method of befriending others with the Gospel that will work in any setting and any culture.

We are ambassadors for Christ, the representatives of our Sovereign in an alien land, negotiating with our fellows to be reconciled to God! The privilege of evangelism has been given to us by the risen Lord. This is not to be done with a slick Madison Avenue salesmanship—not using gimmicks in manipulation of persons. True evangelism in the spirit of Jesus is a loving, respectful, creative, persuasive presentation of the claims of the risen Christ.

Evangelism may be more often by the loving deed rather than by a lengthy presentation of words, but of necessity it includes verbal presentation for no example by itself can adequately represent the truth of Jesus. At best we are witnesses. And in this sense the word interprets the deed and the deed demonstrates the word. As ambassadors we live the Christ-life as the evidence that we are His authentic representatives.

David Bosch, speaking of our being ambassadors in the Spirit of Jesus, gives us a poem from Beatrice Cleveland.

"Not merely by the words you say,
Not only in your deeds confessed
But in the most unconscious way
Is Christ expressed."

"Is it a beautiful smile?
A holy light upon your brow?
Oh, no—I felt His presence while
You laughed just now."

"For me 'twas not the truth you taught,
To you so clear, to me still dim,
But when you came to me you brought
A sense of Him."

"And from your eyes He beckons me
And from your heart His love is shed,
Till I lose sight of you, and see
The Christ instead."
A Spirituality of the Road, p. 57

4

He is the Son of God

"Paul, a servant of Jesus Christ, called to be an apostle, set apart for the gospel of God, which he promised beforehand through his prophets in the holy scriptures, the gospel concerning his Son, who was descended from David according to the flesh and was declared to be the Son of God with power according to the spirit of holiness by resurrection from the dead, Jesus Christ our Lord, through whom we have received grace and apostleship to bring about the obedience of faith among all the Gentiles for the sake of his name, including yourselves who are called to belong to Jesus Christ" (Romans 1:1-6).

"Then I turned to see whose voice it was that spoke to me, and on turning I saw seven golden lamp stands, and in the midst of the lamp stands I saw one like the Son of Man, clothed with a long robe and with a golden sash across his chest. His head and his hair were white as white wool, white as snow; his eyes were like a flame of fire, his feet were like burnished bronze, refined as in a furnace, and his voice was like the sound of many waters. In his right hand he held seven stars, and from his mouth came a sharp, two-edged sword, and his face was like the sun shining with full force. When I saw him, I fell at his feet as though dead. But he placed his right

hand on me, saying, 'Do not be afraid, I am the first and the last, and the living one. I was dead, and see, I am alive forever and ever; and I have the keys of death and of hades'" (Revelation 1:12-20).

The early disciples began carrying out Jesus' commission. They went about proclaiming the NAME, spreading this unique Word across the known world. Paul, too, speaks of God exalting the risen Christ and giving him the NAME that is above every name, and that name is LORD (Philippians 2:10-11). The shortest early Christian creed was simply, "Jesus Christ is Lord." And this is our message, the story and reality of Christ, His birth, life, death, and rising again.

There are basic questions that confront us in this day of increased social pluralism. Why do we believe so particularly in Jesus? Why do we regard His revelation as final? Why do we believe that one comes to God correctly only through Christ? What are the claims of Jesus himself on this matter? How do we come to assurance of faith when answers are based only on the teachings of the Scripture? How could there be a better source than the one closest to the historical account of Jesus, the four Gospels? How other can we understand the nature of the sovereign presence, the Spirit, unless we know Him in and through Jesus, as the Spirit of Jesus?

The story is told that in a university class an agnostic professor was going out of his way to belittle the claims of those who believed in God and affirmed faith in Christ. One of the students was very troubled, and finally raised his hand. "Professor," he asked, "What percent of all of the knowledge in the world would you say that you understand?" The professor thought a bit, and then said, "Well, probably about 3 percent at most." The young man responded, "Has it ever occurred to you that God may be found in the other 97 percent?"

Faith is not built on absolute proof, it is built on evidence. And there is abundant evidence for faith in God, for faith in Christ, and for faith in the Resurrection. Even should one not believe in the inspiration of Scripture, the fact remains that these writings are evidence, for the authority of Scripture must still be recognized similarly as authority in any field of research. In research the scholar seeks to get as close as possible to the event itself. From this perspective even those who do not believe in the inspiration of Scripture must recognize that the Gospels are the authority for Christian faith, one cannot get closer to the Jesus event than in the Gospel records.

A remarkable passage on the Incarnation in the person of Jesus of Nazareth is in the prologue to the gospel of John. "And the Word became flesh and dwelt among us, and we beheld his glory, the glory as of the only begotten of the Father, full of grace and truth" (John 1:14). In the writings of Augustine, he speaks of his interchange with the Neo-Platonists, saying that they could quote the first verses of John's prologue with their perspective of the "Logos principle" being eternal, but they could not quote verse fourteen, "The Logos became flesh and dwelt among us!" The Christ event in the Incarnation is unique to the Christian faith and with it the Crucifixion and resurrection of Christ from the dead.

The Resurrection is the affirmation that Jesus succeeded in all that He promised, that He was who He claimed to be. The Resurrection made clear the meaning of Jesus' words concerning His relation to the Father (Matthew 11:27). Jesus said to Philip, "Have I been with you all this time, Philip, and you still do not know me? Whoever has seen me has seen the Father. Do you not believe that I am in the Father and the Father is in me? Believe me that I am in the Father and the Father is in me; but if you do not, then believe me because of the works themselves. Very truly, I tell you, the one who believes in me will also do the works that I do and, in fact, will do greater works than these, because I am going to the Father. I will do whatever you ask in my name, so that the Father may be glorified in the Son" (John 14:9, 10, 11-13).

Here Jesus affirms that a central privilege of Christian faith is our relationship with God as Father through our relationship with Jesus. One special freedom in this relationship is the privilege of intimacy in prayer. Asking God in the name of Jesus is primarily the recognition that Christ is our Mediator and that we have no merit of our own. His disciples are a people of prayer, because we love Him and especially because we need Him. As believers we converse with Him and we walk with Him in a prayerful relationship. As this makes its unique impact in our lives, we will then be seen as a people of His Resurrection, a people in conversation with Him. The Church has always lived in the fellowship of prayer with the risen Lord, and in our conversation with Him, we actually enter the presence of God. How awesome this privilege!

Paul's statement in Romans is that "Through the Spirit of holiness Jesus Christ our Lord was declared with power to be the Son of God by His Resurrection from the dead" (Romans 1:3). This is Paul's assertion that the resurrection of Christ confirms His divine Sonship. Peter also affirms the same, for in his sermon at Pentecost he declared that the Father raised up Christ (Acts 2:24), giving this as the basis of his declaration that the authority of the gospel message is the risen Christ. In Peter's message to Cornelius, he again stated "God raised him from the dead on the third day and caused him to be seen" (Acts 10:40). This corresponds to what Paul says of the Resurrection as the ultimate sign confirming Jesus' identity as God's Son (Romans 1:3-4). John, in the book of the Revelation, presents Jesus as the risen, triumphant Lord, the Son of God, to be so declared before the entire universe, to the glory of God.

One of the earlier universal expressions of faith, beyond the brief statement, "Jesus is Lord," is the Apostle's Creed. Here in those wonderful declarations we affirm our faith in the one God who has made himself known in the Trinity:

He is the Son of God   71

"I believe in God the Father...
I believe in Jesus Christ His only Son, our Lord...
I believe in the Holy Spirit..."

While the word Trinity is not a biblical term, it is a construct to emphasize the mystery of the one God known in three expressions. It does not speak in the terms I am using, of Oneness and of Threeness. The witness of Scripture is that God identified Jesus as His Son and that Jesus understood His self-identity as being the Son of God. John's golden text says, "For God so loved the world that he gave his only begotten Son that whosoever believeth in Him should not perish but have everlasting life" (John 3:16). God has uniquely come to us in Jesus of Nazareth.

When Jesus was born at Bethlehem, this was His birth as Jesus, but, as the Son of God in divine nature, He has always been with the Father, entering the world as the "Word" made flesh in Jesus. None of us fully understands this mystery. John said, "In the beginning was the Word, and the Word was with God, and the Word was God" (John 1:1-2). This is a mystery, as God himself is "mysterious." This is not the primordial (original first) child of mythology but the eternal Christ of God as historic person.

The mystery of the Incarnation is the great truth that God came to be one with us, one among us. The Virgin Birth is not a doctrine from which we argue that this man with such an unusual birth had to have been divine. Rather, His Virgin Birth means that the eternal Word entered the world in this way to be expressed in solidarity with humanity. We speak of the 'preexistence' of Christ with the Father but not in the same way of a preexistence of Jesus. The birth of the human Jesus as Christ, the Son of God, was a new humanity in that He was without the perversion of sin. In some degree we experience a restoration of genuine humanness in our being regenerated by the Spirit of God.

The historic monistic—believing in only one God—faith in God as the only Lord, for both Jewish and Christian communities,

is found in Moses' words to Israel: "Hear, O Israel: The Lord is
our God, the Lord alone," or literally from the Hebrew, "the Lord
our God is One Lord" (Deuteronomy 6:4). The emphasis of Holy
Scripture is that the Lord is the One, expressed by the Hebrew
word of His majestic Oneness "echad."

One of my professors in Old Testament studies, Dr. G. Irvin
Lehman, was challenged by his Jewish student colleagues in a
class at Hebrew University, New York City, to explain the
Trinity. His answer was, "I will when you explain the difficult
meaning of the Hebrew word, "echad"—One or Oneness?"
This word may not be a simple numerical one but may carry the
greater meaning of Oneness, of Unity (in contrast to polytheism
or the pantheon of Greek gods), a Oneness to which Israel is
witness. Similarly, Christians should not speak of Trinity as a
numerical three but as what Jurgen Multmann emphasizes from
St. John of Damascus, a "parachoric community" of divine sovereign persona. This term, parachoric community, is a strange
term, but it affirms the greatness of God in community as One.
We need to be careful that in our emphasis on Jesus we do not
have a "Jesus only" approach and fail to honor the almighty and
awesome God as Jehovah. Rather we should glorify Yahweh
(God) in His greatness and majesty just as Jesus glorified the
Father with whom He affirmed to be One (John 17:1-5).

In a classic passage in Paul's letter to the Philippians, he
describes the eternal reality of Christ: "Who, though he was in
the form of God, did not regard equality with God as something
to be exploited, but emptied himself, taking the form of a slave,
being born in human likeness. And being found in human form,
he humbled himself and became obedient to the point of death—
even death on a cross. Therefore God also highly exalted him and
gave him the name that is above every name, so that at the name
of Jesus every knee should bend, in heaven and on earth and
under the earth, and every tongue should confess that Jesus Christ
is Lord, to the glory of God the Father" (Philippians 2:6-11).

In reviewing the Christ event from Scripture or from the Apostle's Creed, we speak in theology of the birth-death-rising again of our Lord. Of His birth we speak of the Incarnation, the expression in full humanity of one who was also fully divine. Of the Incarnation we are saying that the Christ became fully human to be God as one with us.

The Incarnation is the greatest affirmation of humanness conceivable. In fact, the Incarnation tells us that God could become human without being sinful. This means that humanness and sinfulness are not synonymous. Jesus is the full expression of the image of God; therefore, we must take seriously the life of Jesus as the Word of God, recognizing that He expresses the character of the new humanity, the new creation, which we share.

As I've noted, in some way the regeneration or re-creation of sinners into new creatures in Christ must be the re-creation of the truly human. To be truly human is by the freedom of resurrection power at work in us now. In the earliest statements about human nature, evil acts are linked to rebellion against God (Genesis 2). Evangelism is the call to end this rebellion. However evangelism is not a cure-all. The work of pastoral counseling and therapy continues as Christians mature. Our salvation is the correction of the rebellion. It is recreating what was lost in humanity—identification with God. In a secular society it is relevant for us to affirm a true humanness, a claim that the one who shares in God's transforming grace is the person who experiences true humanness. We, as Christians in the field of education, have the challenge of interpreting a Christian humanism, something far more comprehensive than secular humanism, for we include the human and the spiritual. On the other hand, secularism in its narrowness excludes the spiritual dimension of fellowship with God.

Jesus shared our humanness, but He also shared the reality of the Divine in the arena of humanness. Apart from Him, our understanding of God would be left to philosophical reflection.

But the contrast between His wholeness and human brokenness and rebellion led to the hostility that cost His life. In accepting crucifixion, Jesus offered the ultimate in self-giving love, (and thereby expressed the substitutionary nature of self-giving, unconditional love). In this love "he tasted death" for each of us, meaning that He literally absorbed human hostility into himself until it killed Him (1 Peter 2:24). In His death He took upon himself the cost of forgiving our sins. In so doing He exposed and emptied violence of its claims for achievement.

This is not the traditional interpretation of the substitutionary view of Christ's death, which focuses on God using Jesus as the penalty for our sin. Such an interpretation presents an offended God punishing Jesus in our place, a very judicial view of revenge for evil. My interpretation is rather a more relational and even psychological interpretation of self-substitution, of a loving God acting in Christ to pay the price of forgiveness in self-giving love (2 Corinthians 5:18). The violence was on the part of humanity against God. In Christ, God absorbed this violence to the death—His nonviolent love absorbing human hostility and speaking back the word of forgiveness. (Note the discussion of this by Denny Weaver in *The Nonviolent Atonement*. I don't agree with Weaver's minimizing of reconciliation and the nature and cost of forgiveness. Eerdmans, pp. 41-44.)

The Resurrection is the certification that God accepted the meaning of the Cross as His answer to the violence of sinners against himself, that in the Resurrection we have the guarantee that we are redeemed. Paul writes, "He was delivered for our offenses and raised again for our justification" (Romans 4:25). The resurrection of Jesus, who unmasked the powers by exposing their violence by His nonviolent love (Colossians 2:15), is now the ultimate victory over sin, death and the Devil, and the key to our reconciliation with God.

One of the most remarkable passages that holds together the life, death and resurrection of Christ is in chapter eight of Paul's letter to the Romans: "For what the law was powerless to do in that it was weakened by our sinful nature, God did by sending his own Son in the likeness of sinful man to be a sin offering. And so he condemned sin in sinful man, in order that the righteous requirements of the law might be fully met in us, who do not live according to our sinful nature but according to the Spirit" (Romans 8:3-4). A special phrase in this text is "that the righteousness of the law might be fulfilled in us." As reconciled people we are now enabled to live in the freedom of His righteousness. We live in the Spirit so that the righteousness to which the law witnessed is now our actual "right relatedness" with God.

We must look at Christology not only from the perspective of the Incarnation and Crucifixion but also from that of the Resurrection and Ascension. In viewing His personhood through the Resurrection we are given the evidence that God has laid His ultimate claim of Sonship on Jesus. The Resurrection is the divine testimony as to who Jesus is and is the divine approval of His life and death. The God who said at Jesus' baptism, "This is my beloved Son in whom I am well pleased" (Matthew 3:17), has in His Resurrection given the ultimate declaration of this Sonship. The Resurrection validates the claims of Jesus, who, for example, spoke of Himself as the "living bread." "Just as the living Father sent me, and I live because of the Father, so whoever eats me will live because of me," (John 6:57). And again, "I and the Father are one" (John 10:30).

To the disciples who "ate of Jesus," the living bread, He was not a prophet in a series of prophets. He was the one and final Word of God. As Karl Barth has emphasized, in reference to God's revelation as self-disclosure, either Jesus Christ was actually God or we don't have a full revelation yet. But, in this full revelation of God in Christ, we are confronted with a God of grace who acts to redeem us, to reconcile us to himself. This is the God we worship, with the disciples of all ages, the God with whom we identify, honestly, even though imperfectly.

While we cannot speak of God adequately because of our sinfulness and our limitations, yet speak we must as an expression of faith while we reach out to God to be identified with Him. God's work of grace is not simply giving us a religion, not even calling us to be religious, but is calling us to himself, reconciling us to himself! We are called to be God's special people, a kingdom of priests (1 Peter 2:10).

In the opening of the Acts of the Apostles, the writer presents the risen Christ appearing and talking with the disciples over a period of forty days. This cannot be overemphasized as historic evidence that Jesus is alive. This is the same Jesus whom they had seen crucified, but He was now risen and to be worshiped as their Lord. As I mentioned earlier, He talked to them about the kingdom of God. This was the same message, a continuation or extension of what He had introduced in His earthly ministry. Also He repeated His promise that they would receive the baptism with the Spirit in a few days, this baptizing by Christ being the first regal act of His sovereign rule following His Ascension (Acts 1:1-8). This remarkable fact we tend to underemphasize— the relation of Pentecost to the Ascension. Pentecost is the assurance that Jesus is at God's right hand.

In Peter's brief sermons in Acts, there are repeated references to the fact that God raised Jesus from the dead and that it is in the name of this Jesus that miraculous power was expressed in the same manner in which it had been demonstrated in the earthly life of Jesus (Acts 2:24, 4:10, 30). In the description of the early church in its prayer assembly we read, "With great power the apostles continued to testify to the resurrection of the Lord Jesus, and much grace was upon them all" (Acts 4:33). Clearly the resurrection of Christ is now at the center of the message of the apostles—for unless Christ lives as sovereign Lord, we are left with only a good example but no reconciling salvation. Our assurance of salvation rests upon the finished work of Christ as our Redeemer, upon His having entered into "the presence of God for us," upon His grace, for "we who have believed do enter into this rest" (Hebrews 4).

In Peter's address to Cornelius, the gentile centurion, Peter emphasized the resurrection of Jesus Christ. The evidence of His resurrected Lordship was expressed in giving the Holy Spirit to the Gentile believers (Acts 10:38-48). This fact Peter used as his argument before the leaders of the Church in Jerusalem as proof that God accepted Gentiles as well as Jews into the community of faith. This was again the proof that Jesus is Lord.

It was this awareness of the deity of Jesus Christ, bursting in upon the minds and lives of the disciples, which transformed them into witnesses of Christ, as Son of God our Savior. The reference to their post-resurrection assembly in the upper room for prayer awaiting Pentecost shows them electing Matthias to take the place vacated by Judas with the specific qualification of his being a witness with them of the Resurrection. The first sermon following Pentecost given by Peter and the sermons that follow in the Acts of the Apostles are messages with significant comment about the resurrected Lord. It is this truth that explains the radical change in the lives of the apostles and explains their giving themselves to the death for the proclamation of the realized kingdom of grace.

In the amazing story of Saul's conversion, we read, "At once he began to preach in the synagogues that Jesus is the Son of God. Saul grew more and more powerful and baffled the Jews living in Damascus by proving that Jesus is the Christ" (Acts 9:20, 22). This change did not come merely by doctrinal insight but by his meeting the risen Christ. In Paul's lengthy sermon at Pisidian Antioch, much of his message is the declaration of the person and resurrection of Jesus the Christ, a fact that he had come to believe by meeting the risen Jesus. This was in spite of the fact that his earlier life at Jerusalem was in full identification with those who rejected Jesus and repudiated the word of Jesus' resurrection (Acts 13:13-52).

Later, at Athens, Paul met with the intellectuals at Mars Hill and his discourse moved from Creation to Redemption to the Resurrection as he presented the nature and acts of God. While some doubted, there were several who became believers (Acts 17:24-34). It is this affirmation that Christ is alive that gives Christianity its unique message. We share in this great line of believers dating back to the time of the apostles as we continue to share and believe the unique message of the risen Christ as Lord.

We must note also the great passages about Christ in Romans 16:25-27, Philippians 2:5-11, and Colossians 1:15-19. Here, in sublime and powerful words, the apostle Paul declares the divine Sonship of Jesus the Christ, "the mystery hidden from long ages past," "he who was in very nature God became in very nature human," "He is the image of the invisible God, in him dwells all of the fullness of the Godhead bodily." These passages are some of the clearest and most emphatic declarations of the divine Sonship of Jesus Christ found in the Epistles. Why from Paul? He was not one of the twelve who might be extending their cause but he, as an unbeliever, had been changed by meeting the risen Christ—hence the importance of his witness.

But the same emphasis appears also in Peter's writings, "Praise be to the God and Father of our Lord Jesus Christ, who in his great mercy he has given us new birth into a living hope through the resurrection of Jesus Christ from the dead" (1 Peter 1:3). Similarly, the conclusions of the four Gospels are specific with detailed accounts of the Resurrection and appearances of the risen Lord. With all of the intellectual questions we may raise about the Resurrection, one thing that is abundantly clear is that the documents declare this as reality. And in the book of Colossians, Paul's insistence that Jesus "is the image of the invisible God" tells us as much about God as it tells us about the Son— God is the kind of God who makes himself known, who gives himself in grace, who calls us to himself in forgiveness and acceptance. God has become visible to us in Jesus of Nazareth, and now, as risen Lord, "He is the head of the body, the church; he is the beginning and the firstborn from among the dead, so that in everything he might have the supremacy" (Colossians 1:18).

It is important, however, that we note the words of Jesus himself, which refer to His relation to the Father. Especially in the Gospel of John, we note the unique expressions of His "Oneness" with the Father in His High Priestly prayer (John 17). Here, while Jesus could have prayed for success and power for His church, He focused on the glory of His relation with the Father, a glory that He has shared and into which He brings His disciples. In Matthew one of the passages from which our teachings about Christ could well begin, Jesus declares: "All things have been committed to me by my Father. No one knows the Son except the Father, and no one knows the Father except the Son and those to whom the Son chooses to reveal him" (Matthew 11:27).

There are many religions in the world in which persons reach groping hands trying to find God. The higher expressions of such a quest are in the philosopher Plato and his quest for the ultimate beautiful, and similarly in Buddha in his search for the light. But these are at best expressions of the human effort to find God. But the good news, the Gospel, is that God has taken the initiative and has come to us. He has made himself fully known in Christ, in whom we have the answer to our quest. We cannot go back to some pre-incarnation level of thought about God, any more than, one in college could go back and live at the level of elementary school. It is because of this full disclosure of God in Christ that we say with Paul, "Other foundation can no one lay than that is laid which is Jesus Christ" (1 Corinthians 3:11).

Who is this Jesus who is risen Lord? What does it mean to affirm that He is at God's right hand? How is He our mediator? How is kingdom-rule being exercised? How is He present with us? How does He impact the world? How is He at work in the world where so many ignore Him and speak of the absence of

God? How is He fulfilling and how will He complete His victory when His method is one of non-coercive love? How, in a materialistic, scientific age, do we think of the immediacy of the Spirit's presence? In what sense is the Messiah the One who has inaugurated a new era, which is literally happening but is spiritual in nature? In what way can the church find its unity as the body of Christ and as the one movement that is transcultural and international? These questions will be developed in succeeding chapters. But note with me the wonderful expression of faith in the beautiful words given to us from the pen of Edmond Bundry of 1884:

> "Thine is the glory, risen, conquering Son;
> Endless is the victory Thou o'er death hast won.
> Angels in bright raiment rolled the stone away,
> Kept the folded grave clothes where the body lay.
>
> Thine is the glory, risen, conquering Son;
> Endless is the victory Thou o'er death hast won.
> Lo! Jesus meets us. Risen from the tomb,
> Lovingly He greets us, scatters fear and gloom;
>
> Let the church with gladness hymns of triumph sing,
> For our Lord now liveth; death hath lost its sting.
> Thine is the glory, risen, conquering Son;
> Endless is the victory, Thou o'er death hast won."

5

Jesus is the One Lord

"I have heard of your faith in the Lord Jesus and your love toward all the saints, and for this reason I do not cease to give thanks for you as I remember you in my prayers. I pray that the God of our Lord Jesus Christ, the Father of glory, may give you a spirit of wisdom and revelation as you come to know him, so that, with the eyes of your heart enlightened, you may know what is the hope to which he has called you, what are the riches of his glorious inheritance among the saints, and what is the immeasurable greatness of his power for us who believe, according to the working of his great power. God put this power to work in Christ when he RAISED HIM FROM THE DEAD and seated him at his right hand in the heavenly places, far above all rule and authority and power and dominion, and above every name that is named, not only in this age but also in the age to come. And he has put all things under his feet and has made him the head over all things for the church, which is his body, the fullness of him who fills all in all" (Ephesians 1:15-23).

In a day of competing religions, we must call each other to look beyond religion itself to the relationship with the God we worship. Having recognized in His Resurrection that Jesus is now known to be God's Son, we therefore know this unique person as our Lord. Christ brought a totally new reality into the human experience. For us, knowing Him as Son of God and as Lord means that our coming to Him is to let God actually be God in our lives. He becomes our Lord, the One who directs us in His will. We become God's children by confessing Jesus as Lord (Romans 10:9). In sermon notes of Wilbur Reese, I found the following bit of humor as a picture of contemporary indifference to God as Sovereign Lord:

> "I would like to buy $3 worth of God, please. Not enough to explode my soul or disturb my sleep, but just enough to equal a cup of warm milk or a snooze in the sunshine. I don't want enough of Him to make me love a person of another race, or pick beets with a migrant. I want ecstasy, not transformation; I want the warmth of the womb, but not a new birth. I want a pound of the eternal in a paper sack. I would like to buy $3 worth of God, please."

As exalted Lord, Jesus stands above all earthly powers; our first loyalty is always to Him. In the days of the Roman Empire, once a year each citizen was to take a pinch of incense and offer it at an altar with the words, "Caesar is Lord." Once the citizen had declared the highest sovereignty to Caesar, the citizen could then worship any god he or she chose, for such a subservient god was now second fiddle and no threat to Caesar. But the Christians had the audacity and the faith to say, "Jesus is Lord!" This they declared in the firm conviction that Jesus was risen and was exalted at God's right hand of power. Jesus is above Caesar and above all other powers, a fact that if understood would correct the civil religion of our day.

In our time and culture we face this very test but in different forms. But on the bottom line we too answer the question, "Who is Lord?" Is it Jesus and His kingdom or the social orders? Jesus or materialism with its status and greed? Jesus or the political forces and the kingdoms of this world? Only, as we keep this issue clear, do we know and experience genuine freedom, the freedom to live by the mandate of Christ above all others. He is our one Sovereign.

The *Apostles' Creed* says, "He ascended into heaven and sits at the right hand of God the Father Almighty, from thence He shall come to judge the living and the dead." From thence! This is His significant position today. He is at the right hand of the Father, the position of Sovereignty, and it is from "thence"— from that position that He will come again.

In John's end time vision, the book of the Revelation, He tells us that the greater view of history is that of the victory of Christ at the right hand of God (chapter one). He is King of kings, and Lord of lords, now. He is sovereign in the universe, and for Christians this has become our declaration of faith and our highest loyalty. We have one Imperial Master, and one Imperial mandate. We need to recognize that history doesn't contain its own fulfillment but it is God's history and He will bring it to its intended conclusion.

The primary significance of the sovereignty of Christ is that He is our Lord to whom we give absolute commitment and do so in the face of other powers. The concept of sovereignty—of Christ over all—is not simply a philosophy that we argue; it is the confession of His sovereign Lordship by which we live. We see this in Peter's early sermon at Pentecost. Peter quotes from Psalm 16:8-11, representing David as speaking of his Lord at God's right hand and declaring that God will not allow His Holy One to see corruption. Interpreting this passage as a word of the resurrection of Christ, Peter declares, "God has raised this Jesus to life and we are all witnesses of the fact. Exalted to the right hand of God, he has received from the Father the promised Holy Spirit and has poured out what you now see and hear"

(Acts 2:32-33). In this wonderful passage, we are given a theology of the exaltation of Christ, of His authority at God's right hand and of His first regal act as the giving of the Holy Spirit to His disciples. This is a theology of the present role of Jesus as Sovereign.

When we accept Jesus as Lord, we accept the *whole* Jesus. We do not accept just part of His person and activity, i.e. His death for us as our Savior, but we accept the whole Jesus. This means that we accept His teaching, mentoring, mediating, and sovereign work as our Master. Jesus came to "seek and to save that which was lost" (Matthew 20:28). In doing so, He acts to turn us back into the "fold of God," to call us home, to incorporate us into God's family and to enable us to live in God's fellowship and by God's priorities. We walk in His will as we "seek first the Kingdom of God and His righteousness" (Matthew 6:33). This calls us to a new relation of freedom among the powers, for Jesus has engaged the powers and is sovereign authority over all (see Walter Wink, *Engaging the Powers*).

In 1981 I was invited by the Oakbrook Executives' Club to address them at a breakfast meeting at the Sheraton in Oakbrook, Ill. Arriving at the Chicago O'Hare Airport the evening before, I stepped outside to catch a hotel limo to the Sheraton. Two other men were standing there chatting, and overhearing them and learning that we were all going to the same hotel, I suggested that we not wait on the limo but hail a taxi and split it three ways. They agreed, we hailed the taxi, and were off. The gentleman who sat with me in the back asked, "Are you here for this agricultural equipment convention tomorrow?"

"No," I said, "I'm here to speak to the Oakbrook Executives' Club."

"What is that?" he asked. I told Him what I knew, that the club had brought speakers from political, economic, and journalistic interests and had now invited me as a theologian.

He said, "And what is your topic?"

"Love, Power, and Freedom," I replied.

At once he said, "They don't fit!"

I smiled and said, "It depends on your definition. If you have power and have no love the power will be tyranny and not freedom, but if you have power and have love there will be freedom, for love doesn't violate or manipulate another."

He was silent for a few moments, and then he said, "Young man, if you could get that message across you would change the world."

I responded, "That is what I'm out to do." Once Jesus' message is understood and His sovereign position affirmed, this can transform our lives and our society.

In 1995 the Mennonite Church adopted a denominational mission statement, "Vision: Healing and Hope." Our conviction expresses a commitment to our sovereign Lord. "God calls us to be followers of Jesus Christ and, by the power of the Holy Spirit, to grow as communities of grace, joy, and peace, so that God's healing and hope flow through us to the world." It is the phrase, *through the power of the Holy Spirit*, which keeps our commitment from being a Jesus-focused legalism. Legalism is always a danger should people profess following "Jesus the example" without recognizing that this relationship is a reality only through the power of the Spirit. But authentic Christian faith is following Jesus. It is worship of the risen sovereign Lord in a fellowship of identification.

In this fellowship we are relating to the Jesus known in history. He lived by the will of God, he is the Word and his lifestyle is the Word of God to us. He lived in the world but not of the world. He could enjoy social engagements without becoming incorporated in the social style. He could enjoy the richness of relationships, including both men and women, without needing sex. He could face opposition without turning to violence. His love was genuine acceptance without His being a wimp, for He could stand up to His opponents and could speak with firmness in judgment. He lived the integrity that He taught.

The apostle John writes, "in the beginning was the Word, and the Word was with God and the Word was God, he was in the beginning with God, all things were made through him and without him was not anything made that was made" (John 1:1-3). The designation "Word" is more than a grammatical vehicle and more than the concept of a principle of universal reason, which the Greek word "Logos" suggests. John writes, the "Word became flesh and made his dwelling among us. We have seen his glory, the glory of the One and only begotten, who came from the Father, full of grace and truth" (John 1:14).

Engaging in evangelistic conversation in this day of pluralism the questions are the same as confronted the early church in the first centuries. How do we respond to the questions, "Who is this Jesus?" and "How does He relate to God?" In 325 the Council of Nicea concluded that Jesus is "Very God, of very God—of the same substance with the Father," the theological affirmations drawn from the declaration of His sovereign position as exalted Lord. In the next period of history the question was, how is this person both human and divine—the issue dealt with at the Council of Chalcedon, 451 A.D. Out of their experience with, and faith in, the living Lord, these church leaders made their affirmations about Jesus. In the Creed they state that in Jesus we recognize two natures, divine and human—unmixed, unconfused, undivided and unaltered. This is the creedal statement, emphasizing the divine and human natures in unity in Jesus the Christ.

Further, for our discussion of the Resurrection it is important that we emphasize a dimension too often lost in the more mystical aspects of thought or of piety: the rule of Christ in the present, the "already" of His kingdom. As Sovereign Lord, He is developing His kingdom now, even while there are future aspects that we affirm as our hope. This present kingdom is given to us by our Lord (Luke 22:29) and is to be engaged by us who are His disciples. The proclamation of the early church had specific references to the "Gospel of the kingdom" (See Acts 20:25, 28:23, 31) and of the present reality of the Kingdom (Romans 14:17 and Colossians 1:13). This kingdom He is creating is a people living by the rule of God. As risen Christ, He is Lord of a kingdom in process, and His Resurrection is the reality to which we witness in a world that does not recognize His rule.

Our Lord rules this kingdom as a spiritual reality in the world now. This kingdom is the present rule of Christ as our Kyrios (Lord) at God's right hand, a rule that is already certifying the victory of God over evil. It is in His Name, in the power of His Name that the work of the kingdom is carried out in the various societies of the world. According to Paul's words to the Corinthians, Jesus will complete this kingdom and then the end will come when He will turn the kingdom over to the Father (1 Corinthians 15:24). What a wonderful word of His victory! It affirms a present engagement in extending His kingdom, an engagement in which we share as His disciples. It gives us identity in the world. We are citizens of the kingdom of heaven now—people who are participating in the new community God is creating.

In late 1526 the Anabaptist leader, Michael Sattler, wrote a letter to Martin Bucer, Reformer of Strasburg, giving twenty reasons why he could not stay in Strasburg and affiliate with the State Church. In this letter there are repeated references to the priorities of the kingdom of God and a call for separation from the orders of this world. This awareness of the present reality of the rule of God in Jesus is one of the unique aspects of the Anabaptist emphasis on a Christ-centered interpretation of the Holy Scripture.

This rule of God, or kingdom, was inaugurated by Jesus as the new order, the new covenant-in-practice. We enter His kingdom by being born into it by the work of the Holy Spirit

(John 3:3, 5). It is a present reality in which we have been inducted, for we have been "translated from the kingdom of darkness into the kingdom of the Son he loves" (Colossians 1:12-14). It is the order by which we live and conduct our lives (Romans 14:17). It is the Gospel, the good news that in a fallen world we can live in resurrection freedom and wholeness, members of the kingdom of Christ (Colossians 1:13, Acts 28:23, 31).

Reformed theology is a sister theology to my tradition, having provided many of the preconditions for the theology of the Anabaptists, but by way of comparison it places a major emphasis on creation rather than kingdom. There has been a long debate (as referred to earlier in reference to Oliver O'Donovan, *Resurrection and Moral Order*, p. 15), over the "ethics of creation" and the "ethics of the kingdom." But as O'Donovan says in his analysis, this division is not acceptable. "The very act of God which ushers in His kingdom is the resurrection of Christ from the dead, the reaffirmation of creation. A kingdom ethics which was set up in opposition to creation could not possibly be interested in the same eschatological kingdom as that which the New Testament proclaims. A creation ethics, on the other hand, which was set up in opposition to the kingdom, could not possibly be evangelical ethics, since it would fail to take note of the good news that God had acted to bring all that He had made to its fulfillment. In the resurrection of Christ, creation is restored, and the kingdom of God dawns. Ethics that begin from this point may sometimes emphasize the newness, sometimes the primitiveness of the order that is there affirmed. But it will not be tempted to overthrow or deny either in the name of the other" (Ibid. p. 15).

A further unique account of the authority of His name, of the power of the risen Christ expressed through His apostles, is the story of their imprisonment and miraculous escape (Acts 5:12-42). Upon their preaching and healing in the name of Jesus they were arrested by the Sanhedrin and imprisoned. Early the next morning the officers went to bring them to trial only to find the prison locked but the cell empty! News came that the apostles were in the temple preaching, and the guard went and brought them without violence. It was in their trial that Gamaliel, a doctor of the law, Paul's major professor in his studies, gave a speech that called for a "wait and see" posture to discern whether this work be of God or of man. We have no record that Gamaliel ever examined or followed the evidence himself. But most significant for this study is the message of Peter at their trial:

"The God of our fathers raised Jesus from the dead—whom you had killed by hanging him on a tree. God exalted him to his own right hand as Prince and Savior that he might give repentance and forgiveness of sins to Israel. We are witnesses of these things, and so is the Holy Spirit, whom God has given to those who obey him" (Acts 5:30-32). Peter's statement clearly puts Christ at center and Jesus, the Servant of God, has been exalted by God to the 'right hand' of authority as Prince and Savior! Jesus has been designated Lord!

Earlier, Stephen, in a vision during his martyrdom, saw an expression of this exaltation and authority of Jesus. The passage reads, "But Stephen, full of the Holy Spirit, looked up to heaven and saw the glory of God, and Jesus standing at the right hand of God. 'Look,' he said, 'I see heaven open and the Son of Man standing at the right hand of God'" (Acts 7:54-56). It has been noted that the vision of Jesus standing rather than sitting is an expression of how the risen Christ identifies with His own here on earth. He was standing, looking down at Stephen, a vision in which Jesus identified himself with His church and with what was happening to His servant.

In the account of Philip preaching in Samaria, the Lordship of Christ is linked to the reality of the kingdom. "But when they believed Philip as he preached the good news of the kingdom of God and the name of Jesus Christ, they were baptized" (Acts 8:12). Significantly, the nature of the kingdom is seen here as cross-cultural, in the extension of the Gospel beyond the Jewish community to the Samaritans. And just as there had been a Jewish Pentecost, so now there was a Samaritan Pentecost as God's certification of equality in grace. Similarly, when Peter preached to Cornelius (Acts 10), there was a Gentile Pentecost as certification that Gentiles were also accepted by grace in the kingdom of God. Jesus as Lord is giving His Spirit to those who covenant with Him.

In the story of Saul's conversion on the Damascus Road, it is his confrontation with the risen Christ, head of the church, which brought him to faith (Acts 9:5, 17). In his vision Jesus identified himself with the church in the words, "Why do you persecute me?" Immediately in his sermons Paul began to prove from the Scriptures (the Old Testament), that Jesus is the Christ (Acts 9:22), and this theme is central in his sermons throughout the accounts in Acts (18:4-10, 26:15-18, 28:23, 31), as well as in his epistles.

A key passage on the present aspects of the kingdom is in the letter to the Colossians, as quoted earlier, "God has translated us (now) from the kingdom of darkness into the kingdom of his Son" (Colossians 1:13). A remarkable passage in the letter to the Ephesians deals explicitly with the exalted role of Jesus, with his position "above all authority, power, and dominion, and every title that can be given, not only in the present age but also in the one to come" (Ephesians 1:17-23). Here Paul says that God has placed all things under His feet and has appointed Him to be head over all things. In effect, the principalities and powers find it compelling to look in on His church to see what Christ is doing, how He is working in the world today (Ephesians 3:10-11). To the Romans, Paul wrote, "The kingdom of God is not meat and drink, but righteousness, and peace and joy in the Holy Spirit" (14:17). This is to say the kingdom is not a matter of ritualistic observance of religious feasts but a spirit of life, in which we live in the will of the King.

As exalted Lord, He is our High Priest, our Mediator, the One who certifies before the angelic hosts of heaven and the representatives of hell, that God has acted in our redemption (Hebrews 4:14-16). The writer of Hebrews declares that our salvation is sure and complete because Jesus "always lives to intercede" for us (Hebrews 7:25). As the ultimate meaning of Jesus' sacrifice, the writer says that the risen Christ now "appears in the presence of God for us" (Hebrews 9:24).

It has been a real challenge for me in seeking to understand how God expresses His sovereignty in our lives and yet respects—even creates—our freedom. I believe that we must understand as clearly as possible the manner in which God, as Father, has expressed His sovereignty in the long sweep of history. We must study the actions of God for the thousands of years before Jesus of Bethlehem. But it is necessary for me to define my understanding of sovereignty.

I understand the sovereignty of God to be like self-determination in a person. God, our Sovereign, is the one self-determined Being in the universe and He acts out of His own nature, acting consistently with himself. God is sovereign and this means He alone determines His course of action and that His action is consistent with His very "God-ness." God could, in His sovereignty, as Luther suggested, have kicked the world to pieces; God could have long ago exterminated the Devil. But God is acting in a different pattern by sovereign self-determination, consistent with himself in love and mercy and justice. God's action uniquely overcomes evil with good, exposing its perversions and in so doing demonstrates the wholeness of His love, mercy, justice, and grace in a manner that respects the freedom He has given to us.

As the Son of God, it follows that Jesus expresses His sovereignty as exalted Lord in the same manner in which God the Father has expressed His sovereignty. Jesus chooses to work in a different manner than acting in a deterministic way and expresses

His holiness and love over against evil and its perversion. His redemption means exposing evil for what it is and overcoming it. Jesus' victory is not by exercising His superior power and destroying evil through this power. His victory comes by expressing love and holiness, and He did this at the stupendous cost of shedding His own blood on the cross. As John R. W. Stott states, "Jesus absolutely refused to retaliate. By his self-giving love for others, he overcame evil with good" (Romans 12:21). "By his obedience, his love and his meekness he won a great moral victory over the powers of evil" (*The Cross of Christ*, p. 235).

Jesus said, in the Garden of Gethsemane, that He could have called for twelve legions of angels and confronted evil with superior power. But evil is defeated by exposing it to the holiness of divine love. Like the Father, Jesus expressed superior quality, exposing evil by expressing divine holiness and love. Jesus went to Calvary to meet and expose the terrible nature of evil and at the same time overcoming it with the marvelous expression of self-giving love.

From this perspective, we see a real difference between righteousness and rebellion. The expression of God's grace exposes the deep perversions of sin and of evil. Evil is darkness in contrast to light. In the light evil is exposed and is overcome in the victory of divine love. The final judgment of evil will be when God removes His presence, withdraws His goodness, and leaves evil to itself alone—it will be its own hell. Once God withdraws everything that issues from His goodness—even from the arena in which evil exists as a parasite—there will be nothing left but evil itself and that will be its ultimate self-destruction in which evil is only a "bottomless pit," the "black hole" of the universe!

When the question is asked in the face of happenings or expressions of evil in the world, "Where is God?" or "Where is the sovereign Lord?" the implication of the question is that if God is sovereign, He should move in and overcome evil by an exercise of His superior power. But this is not the manner in which God works to overcome evil. If He should act in such a manner in any situation He would thereby destroy the integrity of His own holiness. Such action of destroying evil by his superior power would make meaningless his action through the ages of overcoming evil by his superior goodness. Evil is actually overcome by exposing it for what it is and at the same time demonstrating God's holiness and love.

Now, if our Lord as risen and exalted Sovereign chooses to work in holiness and love, the Holy Spirit who indwells those of us who follow Him will lead us to live by the same self-giving, sacrificial love. This is the spirit and the manner in which the Holy Spirit overcomes evil through us. By our being expressions of His transforming grace we become a word of grace to the world and thereby represent redemption as something real. We, who are in Christ, are the body of Christ, a presence for and of Jesus in the world. By the quality of our nonviolent spirit and behavior, we confront evil with the witness that God's way is infinitely superior. The basis of Christian ethics is primarily our belonging to Christ and living by the same spirit and life to which He bound himself. This is a theology of love and nonviolence. We are peacemakers in the world, agents of compassion and service as witnesses to the new life in Christ.

Jesus fulfilled the righteous demands for our salvation and we live by faith in the completed work of Christ for our redemption. He is our reconciler, the one in whom we are given a saving relationship with God. Now that the redemptive work is accomplished there is a "rest" for the people of God, a rest in that we cease from our own works by trusting in His work (Hebrews 4:1-11). Our eyes are on Jesus, not on ourselves or on our achievements. They are on our Redeemer who "sat down on the right hand of the throne of God" (Hebrews 12:2). Our salvation, our membership in God's kingdom is the reality for a Christian lifestyle. It is also our hope, as we celebrate His victory, affirming our belief in His present rule and our anticipation of the future, the "not yet" of the kingdom of God (Revelation 1:17-18, 12:10-12).

Theologian Jurgen Moltmann, in lectures once at Goshen Biblical Seminary, Indiana, emphasized the nature of discipleship as living out the relationship we have with the kingdom of Christ. Moltmann says, "If Christ is Lord, then already all power in heaven and on earth is given to Him. It also follows that, in reading Romans 13, we should not isolate this chapter from its context to formulate a Christian view of the state, the chapter must be seen in the context of what precedes and follows, addressing how Christians should respond to evil, and specifically to government, and not be seen as a theological umbrella to cover or justify the acts of the state" (*Following Jesus Christ*, pp. 46-47).

I concur with Moltmann in his interpretation of Romans 13, but I must also point out another factor. The statement of the apostle Paul: "The powers that be are ordained of God," should be read as saying God ordains; therefore, God is still above the powers! The powers are ordained of God! At times we can only respond with the apostles by saying, "We ought to obey God rather than man."

The Anabaptist/Mennonite position of nonresistance, of being defenseless as a sign of our discipleship, is based on our firm conviction that there is one eternal mandate—that of our eternal Lord, Jesus Christ. We are called to stand with the risen Christ as a strategy of peace. We are called to stand with Michael Sattler, author of the *Schleitheim Confession* (pp. 269-272), who at his trial at Rottenburg on the Neckar River and his martyrdom in 1527, answered the question of how to defend against the danger of the Turks, "Extend Christian love, live by nonviolent (defenseless) love!" This is positive action and relevant today, as we ask the questions of how to defend against terrorism. Love is active. Love takes the initiative to build bridges of understanding and respect.

Living in relationship with our one Sovereign we are free in relation to all other powers. Gladys Aylward, who wanted to go to China as a missionary and was turned down by a mission board in London, went as a self-appointed missionary. Hers is an amazing story, presented in the film, *Inn of the Sixth Happiness*. After some years of identifying with the Chinese people, upon the invasion by the Japanese, she was told by her friend, a Chinese army officer, she would need to be prepared to take the lives of enemies. In her inimitable style she said, "When my choice has to be between the wishes of my country and the will of God, I know which to choose."

Such a stance can only be taken when we have resolved the fear of death and can face issues with the awareness that we don't *have* to live, we can die. Rather than give up the integrity of our faith, we can choose this stance, in the grace of God and in the hope of eternal life. The apostles proclaimed with the resurrection of Christ the resurrection of humankind as well! But the resurrection of humankind without a renewal of Creation would not be a full gospel message. There is no meaningful way of speaking of faith in our future resurrection unless one also believes in the fact and power of God's creative work.

The Resurrection directs our attention to our future but also back to the Creation and to the act of the Creator. In doing so we speak of the order and the coherence in which creation is composed at the hand of the Creator. It is the Creator, God, who is able to raise us up. In fact, resurrection power is contingent upon creation power. Creation and Resurrection are joint affirmations that all things are "for Him" and "in Him," as Paul writes in the Colossians (1:15-17). (O'Donovan deals at some length with this subject in *Resurrection and Moral Order*, chapter 2, "Created Order," pp. 31-52).

Perhaps a theology of Creation and a theology of kingdom can be harmonized by a joint emphasis on the ultimate purposes of our sovereign God. His will of shalom for all people calls us to celebrate wholeness. For the human family this includes reconciliation, justice, peace, and love. In regards to the created order, Christians are called to ecological integrity; we are called to handle the earth in a manner consistent with God's intention. We should use it but not abuse it—engage its resources for the general well-being of all peoples—but preserve its resources for the generations to come. No single generation owns this planet. We are its custodians—stewards who answer to God.

A theology of kingdom will not disregard the Creation and a theology of Creation will always ask of the Creator the intent and meaning of His rule! We are to be fruitful in the world—not ruled by the material but under God ruling in the use and distribution of resources. This calls us to share resources with the peoples of the world. No Christian can rest comfortably without helping to deal with the gap between those of poverty and those of plenty, the gap between the "haves" and the "have nots," the powerful and the powerless.

A prophetic word from the church is to call those in power to the responsibility of justice for all people, to serve the poor as well as the powerful and to respect the dignity and value of each person alike. In the community of faith the prophetic calls us to equity and loving service to all peoples alike—the privileged and deprived—to enable all persons to enjoy the richness of God's benefits toward us. We are called to love as the practical working out of the idea of self-giving, to justice as the means of setting things right, and to peace as the practice of loving one's neighbor as one's self. As disciples, we are committed to equity and mutuality. We are not so much what we profess, but what we love. And we live in His love on this side of the Resurrection but in the fellowship of divine love.

6

Since the Resurrection

"Now on that same day two of them were going to a village called Emmaus, about seven miles from Jerusalem, and talking with each other about all these things that had happened. While they were talking and discussing, Jesus himself came near and went with them, but their eyes were kept from recognizing him. And he said to them, 'What are you discussing with each other while you walk along?' They stood still, looking sad. Then one of them, whose name was Cleopas, answered him, 'Are you the only stranger in Jerusalem who does not know the things that have taken place there in these days?' He asked them, 'What things?' They replied, 'The things about Jesus of Nazareth, who was a prophet, mighty in deed and word before God and all the people, and how our chief priests and leaders handed him over to be condemned to death and crucified him. But we had hoped that he was the one to redeem Israel. Yes and besides all this, it is now the third day since these things took place. Moreover, some women of our group astounded us. They were at the tomb early this morning, and when they did not find his body there, they came back and told us that they had indeed seen a vision of angels who said that he was alive. Some of those who were with us went to the tomb and found it just as the women had said; but *they did not see him.' Then he said to them, 'Oh, how foolish you are, and how slow of heart to believe all that the prophets have declared! Was it not necessary that the Messiah should suffer these things and then enter into his glory?' Then beginning with Moses and all the prophets, he interpreted to them the things about himself in all the scriptures"* (Luke 24:13-27).

What a riveting and amazing story presented to us in this text! How timeless the significance of this appearance of the risen Christ to these persons on the Emmaus road! Jesus talked with them and yet in their grief and quandary they were prevented from recognizing Him. But the conversation is pivotal. It is one of the greater presentations of the difference the Resurrection made for the Disciples of Christ—a difference in faith perspective, a difference in relationship with the Lord, and a difference in reading the Scripture.

A gentleman drove to the mall to pick up his wife as she came from her work. He was early and so he ran his car through the carwash. Parking near the curb where he would meet his wife, he got out and began wiping his car. He noticed a man coming across the parking lot, who was shabby, dirty and unshaven. He ignored him and continued wiping his car, but the man came over and sat on the curb by the bus stop and watched him. He glanced at the "bum" now and then, and finally the derelict commented, "That is a nice car." The man smiled and said, "Yes it is, I enjoy it." Then looking at the "bum," noting his appearance in poverty, thinking, 'this man doesn't even have money for a bus fare,' he said to him, "Do you need something?" The man simply responded, "Don't we all?" The words got to him, "Don't we all?" He went over and handed the fellow much more than the bus fare, enough for several meals, and the man thanked him. But as he went back to his car, he kept thinking of those few words, "Don't we all?" words that became a gift to him of recognizing how much each of us alike is in need of grace.

As we read the Scripture, we need to hear it in grace. We must recognize that we read it from this side of the event, this side of His Resurrection. We read it from the fulfillment of Scripture in the victory of the risen Christ. In this freedom, we must recognize an inerrancy of meaning and not be tied to a proof-text legalism that claims that there is no error in the words. Our interpretation of the "Word written" is shaped by our understanding of the "Word in Jesus." In this account we recognize God's "promise" (in the OT) and "fulfillment" (in the NT) center in the life, death, and resurrection of Christ. God's act of reconciling us to himself is victoriously fulfilled in the resurrection. Paul writes, "He was delivered for our offenses and raised again for our justification" (Romans 4:25). We cannot focus our thinking by going back before Jesus' birth or the Resurrection, for if we seek honestly to truly hear God's word it is in the risen Christ.

Peter's first sermon in the book of Acts illustrates the way Peter himself was changed by this reality. The resurrection of Christ changed his personal life but also changed his way of reading and interpreting the Scriptures (See Acts 2:14-40). This change came from "being born again by a living hope through the resurrection of Jesus Christ from the dead" (1 Peter 1:3).

The resurrection of Jesus helps us to understand faith personally and to read the Scriptures differently than we would if Scripture was only value statements without relationship with a personal God through the Christ. In a practical way, this faith causes us to read the two Testaments of the Bible differently, even while seeing their grand unity. The whole of Scripture focuses the fulfillment of the Old in the New. The Old Testament is not "the Hebrew bible," nor is it to be read primarily as law, but it is a part of the whole and helps us to see God's self-disclosure finally made clear in Christ. It is calling us to a new relationship with God in Christ. We now understand that God's grace illuminates His law, demonstrating that God is not indifferent to the people of His love.

When the meaning of the Resurrection impacted the disciples, it changed the way they saw the "First" Testament. This freedom enabled them to see the reconciling grace of God in a new way expressed in Christ. In Jesus' message to the two disciples on the Emmaus road we have a remarkable exercise in interpretation. The text says he "unfolded to them in all of the scriptures the things concerning himself." This interpretation now becomes the pattern for the disciples and for the writers of the New Testament Scriptures. It is also the guide for us as we interpret the whole of the Scripture. We now interpret the Old Testament through the full word of God expressed in Jesus the Christ. This is not a rejection of the Old Testament but is a recognition that it stands in relation to the New Testament. The Old Testament is promise—the New Testament is fulfillment. We also hear Jesus say, "It has been said...but I say unto you," giving us its full meaning. The Resurrection changes our understanding of the expected Messiah, clearly not primarily as an earthly king but as the "suffering servant" who has become the exalted Lord (Philippians 2:5-12).

In the eighth chapter of Hebrews, the writer outlines how the new covenant supersedes the old. Here the writer, writing with Paul's thinking but no doubt it was by someone writing for Paul, (perhaps Priscilla), clearly presents Jesus as our supreme High Priest. Above the priests of the old covenant, the ministry Jesus has received is as superior to theirs as the covenant of which He is mediator is superior to the old one, and it is founded on better promises. "For if there had been nothing wrong with that first covenant, no place would have been sought for another" (Hebrews 8:6-7).

Hermeneutics, the exercise of biblical interpretation, is more than the study of the text. It looks at the culture in which it was composed, the languages and their development as symbols that pass on meaning, and the context and interpretation of what the writer was sharing. In addition, it is above all, reflection on what it means to read the text in light of God's full expression in Christ. Each of us must recognize and evaluate the elements that condition our reading of the Bible—that is, what we bring to the Bible in theology, faith, culture, philosophy, etc.

The fact that one believes in the full inspiration of Scripture does not mean that one can ignore the issues of interpretation and simply quote the words. Our use of the inspired Word calls for very honest and very serious recognition of the principles of interpretation. Hermeneutics deals with theological presuppositions—those thought traditions that shape our hearing of the text. In fact, recognizing our theological presuppositions is not only essential but is one of the more difficult aspects of hermeneutics. We need to be very honest about our perspectives if we are to truly meet the Lord beyond our presuppositions, be they conservative or liberal. And may I say, the most demanding intellectual task is to be an "avant-garde" conservative, taking seriously the whole range of historical interpretation and thought. Being a liberal is quite freewheeling, individualistic, and, in comparison, rather easy.

Or to take quite a different illustration on the New Testament use of the Old Testament, Paul, in Romans, sees believers as the people of faith who are the true Israel. Yet the Christian Zionist movement among very conservative Christians read Old Testament promises to Israel before the coming of the Messiah and intended to prepare the way for the Messiah as promises to yet be fulfilled for the political good of Israel. They would do well to read Leviticus 25:23 where God says to Israel, "The land is mine and you are but aliens and my tenants." And in chapter 26, God repeatedly warns them, that if they are disobedient, He will take the land away and grant it a sabbatical of rest, even under foreign occupation—a rest that they violated. This question of whose land is Palestine continues to divide Christian interpreters as well as dividing between Israelis and Palestinians. A sense of God's love for all peoples alike, of God's justice and equity for all, brings a different perspective to the way in which we could work with the Middle East. An equivalent aid by other nations to Palestinians similar to what is being done for the Israelis would have radically altered the tensions and development.

The historical Jesus is now the risen Jesus Christ our Lord and we read the Bible through our understanding of Him in His Resurrection. His earthly life and teaching is our guide in knowing Him—even though now we know Him in a faith identity. We know Him as our contemporary who is at God's right hand. We have a new name for God; He is the God who raised Jesus Christ from the dead! The new humanity, new creation, is expressed in the risen Christ and He promises us that this new humanity will be given to us as our fulfillment but is also the new community for meaningful relationships.

The Christian church is built on Christ as its one foundation; it exists by its faith in Christ. As our one foundation for faith, He is the image of the invisible God, the one Savior and Lord, the one Mediator between God and humanity. As we confess Jesus as our Lord, He is our Messiah (the Christ); He is head of the church, the Redeemer in whom we have our salvation. As we study Christ, we should do so moving from Jesus' life to His Resurrection, for we live in a world where the same Jesus who walked and taught in Galilee and Judea is now our contemporary and our Lord!

A resurrection Christology means that we share solidarity with Him as risen Lord. We as believers are a "Jesus people." Through His Word we can talk with Him, we can walk with Him, we can share in love of Him and in service for Him. Paul wrote to the Colossians, "If you are risen with Christ, seek the things that are above where Christ sits on the right hand of God" (Colossians 3:1). This freedom, this new order of life, is in relationship with Christ. Our focus is now set on things above.

Paul tells us that our "citizenship is in heaven" (Philippians 3:20). This is crucial for us today. We are "resident aliens."

When we say, "Jesus is Lord," we are not simply quoting a creedal statement of who He is, but in this confession we are saying, "Jesus is my Lord." This confession breaks the tyranny of any other claim and sets us free in grace for the kingdom of Christ. We are free to be in the world but not of the world, good citizens but not "yes persons" who fail to challenge social and political systems. The central aspects of the "good news" of the gospel are: the Incarnation and its expression of the will of God; the Crucifixion and its claim that the redeemed belong to the Redeemer; the Resurrection and Ascension of Christ as sovereign Lord. Paul wrote, "If Christ has not been raised, your faith is futile and you are still in your sins" (1 Corinthians 15:17).

Speaking of how Abraham's "faith was reckoned to him for righteousness," Paul writes, "It will be reckoned to us who believe in him who raised Jesus our Lord from the dead, who was handed over to death for our trespasses and was raised again for our justification" (Romans 4:24-25). In His life we have the basis for assurance of reconciliation. By believing in Him we are made new persons.

In 1999 assisting my wife Esther in a conference for artists she convened in Bulgaria, I was impressed by the words of persons who had recently come out of atheistic communism, "Since I am a believer," "Before I was a believer," or "Now that I am a believer!" How refreshing! How focused! This immediacy of faith was very essential in their lives and decision-making. This was a totally new freedom, and this should be our identity, believers!

The Resurrection of Christ declares that Jesus is victor over sin, death, and the Devil. The Resurrection is the ultimate assurance of this victory. We live in a world where, although Satan is active, he is defeated. Terrorists may terrorize but temporarily— Jesus is victor. Violence may be a universal evil, but love is the one power that will live on. Nonviolent engagement can expose and go beyond the limits of violence. This is the message of the cross! As Martin Luther King said, "Hate cannot drive out hate, it takes love to do that."

By the power of His Spirit and also in His spirit or manner we are enabled to minister to persons oppressed by evil in the name of Christ. The demonic is vanquished. James writes, "Resist the Devil, and he will flee from you" (James 4:7). In some Christian communities there is a prominent emphasis on "spiritual warfare," but this is more mystical than a genuine confrontation by nonviolent love. I would caution those who engage this ministry that they can do so only in the victory of Christ. We should avoid conversing with the Devil or regarding him as a divine power! The Devil is no second God! Our Lord defeats him. Our victory over demonic power is by standing in the victory of Christ.

As Paul writes, "Put on the whole armor of God so that you can take your stand against the Devil's schemes. For our struggle is not against flesh and blood, but against the rulers, against the authorities, against the powers of this dark world and against the spiritual forces of evil in the heavenly realms" (Ephesians 6:11-12). Our stance is one of covenant with Christ as Victor. We stand in freedom from all powers that are not with Christ. We will be tempted but we take our stand in solidarity with Jesus and He secures the victory—our freedom.

The fact is, the resurrection is central, not peripheral. It is primary, not secondary. "Every book in the New Testament declares or assumes that Christ rose from the dead" (Richardson, p. 193). Again Alan Richardson, in *"An Introduction to the Theology of the New Testament,"* says, "Christianity is a religion of miracle, and the miracle of Christ's Resurrection is the living center and object of Christian faith" (p. 197). Emil Brunner asserts: "On the resurrection everything else depends" (*Letter to the Romans*, p. 131). This means, as we study Christ, that we should view the whole of the life of Jesus of Nazareth through His Resurrection. The historical Jesus is affirmed by the

Resurrection to be the full Word of God; He is the "Word (who) became flesh and dwelt among us" (John 1:14).

Our discipleship means a daily following of Christ, a "nachfolge Christi." This is solidarity with the risen Jesus. It is not imitating Jesus but is consciously and freely identifying with Him, our Savior, our Reconciler, our Mentor, and our Enabler. Christian experience is to walk with Jesus in life. This identification with Christ is the energy for a redeemed community.

The reality of the Resurrection presence is the common fellowship of the new community, of our life together in the church of which Christ is the Head. Jesus promised, "Where two or three are gathered together in my name there I am in the midst of them." This is the essential nature of the church. His presence moves us beyond being merely a religious club to actually being the "body of Christ." God has "made him the head over all things for the church, which is his body, the fullness of him who fills all in all" (Ephesians 1:22-23). Even our family order is comparable, as Christ is Guardian (Head) of the church so the husband is guardian for the wife (Ephesians 5:23), self-giving for the welfare of the other.

As Christian thinkers, we should more consistently emphasize the implications of the Resurrection, the Ascension, and exaltation of Christ at the right hand of God. Too little is said of what this means now for us, as members of His body or of His kingdom, the expression of the rule of God in the present. His kingdom of grace and glory is experienced today in the glory of our relationship with Him. He is not a dictator in control of our lives, but He is present and always there for us.

The Scripture says that God has given Him to be head of the church, to carry out His mission for the world. To think of this politically, Christ is our highest authority and the church is His primary movement in the world. To think socially, the church crosses all national lines, as well as all cultural, class, and racial lines. The kingdom of God is trans-national, trans-cultural, and trans-racial. All peoples are called into faith, into a fellowship of equity and of mutuality. To think theologically, He is Creator and guardian of the church, and we are to be responsibly Christ-centered in our perspectives of faith.

As a part of His body, each one of us finds our character, our calling, and our community in this new fellowship. As we share in the redeemed community, living as members of the kingdom of God, we experience the victory of the exalted Christ and His rule at the right hand of the Father. He is our Lord and our King, both now and coming in the culmination of His work and rule. His is a kingdom of grace and of glory. The kingdom in grace is given to us now in anticipation of the full expression of His kingdom in glory. As the Apostles' Creed says, "From THENCE He shall come..." that is, from that unique place at God's right hand or that highest position. He is sovereign Lord now and He will come again as supreme Lord. He is the same Jesus who lived and taught the will of God among us. Our hope is the future fulfillment of the kingdom which He introduced and which He is even now expressing through the church in and to the world.

My wife Esther and I had the opportunity, among other rich experiences, of working in Washington, D.C., for fourteen years. In the context of both political and inner-city relationships, we tested this theology. We went to Washington, D.C., in May of 1981 and planted a church from scratch on Capitol Hill. We invited another couple, Curt and Judy Ashburn, who were coming to Washington for another program, to join us in the work. Together we had the joy of seeing a congregation develop through the work of the Spirit as an emerging community of disciples. The congregation has continued to grow in size and quality, with transitions in leadership, in multi-denominational and interracial developments.

One of our tenets of faith in this church was the concept of the "Third Way," meaning a way that is neither "liberal" nor "conservative" but the way of the kingdom. This approach calls for us to select from either "right" or "left" and reject from either "right" or "left" on the basis of our relation to the kingdom of Christ. But if you should politicize this Third Way as a political party, in doing so, you would destroy its uniqueness. The way of the kingdom will liberate us from polarizing and from the dominance of any humanism (belief in human ability to conquer all). Conservative Francis Schaffer has said, "A conservative humanism is just as wrong as a liberal humanism." With the diversity within the congregation, if one side pressed the other side to their position, they would violate unity, which is a spirit of relation that goes beyond sameness! Genuine unity is only possible with diversity.

This Third Way approach made us conscious daily of the need to discern the will of our Lord Christ on issue after issue. In our social and political conversation, the old approach of right or left, which is followed by so many, is in no way adequate. Further, as Christians, we need to understand that a conservative theology does not mean that we must have a conservative political or social view. Actually, a conservative theology with a high view of Scripture, a belief in the deity and resurrection of Christ, and a belief in the primacy of the kingdom of God means that we must hold other systems under question. We relate to other systems in freedom for selectivity, that is, we are free to decide what roles are legitimate for a disciple of Christ. A conservative theology should be expressed as progressive and innovative. Further, we need a new understanding of community, a new interpretation of our social and political responsibilities in light of our world context.

In Paul's first letter to the Corinthians, he makes reference to Jews, Greeks, "or the church of God" (1 Corinthians10:30). Here is a significant notation of this third group, the church of God! We are a church of this Third Way, the way of the kingdom of Christ. In a politically-divided time, this emphasis is helpful in our mission, for it frees us from being either rightist or leftist, but to be a non-partisan people of a Third Way, the way of the kingdom. We are free to follow our Lord and select from either "right" or "left" and to reject from either; this is a way of freedom in Christ. According to the "Letter to Diognetes," A.D.150, the early Christians were recognized as a "Third Race." This was used as a taunt by Aristides, and taken up by Ceclus. But the insult became something of an insight, according to Adolph Harnack in *Mission and Expansion of Christianity in the First Three Centuries* (Book 2, Ch.7). We are not a third race, but we are a people of a Third Way.

In most systems of evangelical theology, there is a prominent and good emphasis on creation, the fall, the redemption of humanity by the cross, and consummation divine purpose with Christ's return. But this leaves something crucial out, for it fails to adequately emphasize Christ's new community between the cross and the consummation of His coming. There is too little emphasis on the risen Christ functioning as head of the church as His special redeemed community in today's world. He is head of the church now, its guardian, its Lord and Master, our one supreme authority. Christ is at work now creating His kingdom.

In a significant volume, *The Resurrection and Moral Order*, Oliver O'Donovan points out an unfortunate division between a "Theology of Creation" and a "Theology of Kingdom," a division that needs to be resolved. Those who hold to a theology centered in creation tend to minimize the role of the kingdom of Christ in its present extension of the "rule of God." The two theologies can be brought together. "In the resurrection of Christ, creation is restored and the kingdom of God dawns" (Eerdmans, p. 15). Further, O'Donovan points to the effect of this Resurrection power on ethics, with a relationship between creation and kingdom, that we need to bring these two views of ethics together in our thinking, and in doing so, we will find the higher ethic of loving faithfulness—a relationship of spirit and wisdom, above law, and legalistic obedience.

Before leaving this chapter, a brief review will emphasize Christian theology as based on activity God initiates. Divine disclosure is not simply to provide us with knowledge about God but is to express His call for us to identify with Him in the covenant of grace. I have said previously that God's revelation, while encompassing the whole of Scripture, finds its full expression in Jesus Christ. Similarly, Richard Lintz writes, "There is a fundamental direction to the conversation with God. First, He speaks through the unfolding of the history of redemption recorded in Scripture, which reaches a climax in the person and work of Christ, and in Him we hear God speak. As we listen to the message, we may understand ourselves anew. The message originates with God, and takes seed in our minds and hearts, and only then do we comprehend that God is Lord over redemptive history and that we have a particular role to play in this history" (*The Fabric of Theology*, p. 66).

The field of theology is replete with many studies of the historical Jesus, studies of the Jesus of the various writers: Mark's Jesus, Matthew's Jesus, Luke's Jesus, John's Jesus, the Jesus of Paul, and the Jesus of the writer of Hebrews. Scholars even search for a proposed source called "Q" which they believe was the basis for Mark and Matthew. We should see these as different presentations that find their grand unity in the essence of a personal revelation. Too often scholars concentrate on the differences in the pictures rather than the basic agreements. For example, the redaction (which means editing) approach sees the early church experience being read back into the accounts attributed to Jesus so much that they minimize Jesus' contribution. Since the church was created by the resurrected Jesus there is of course a valid "reading back" from the post-resurrection insights, for the Jesus who proclaimed the gospel has now *become* the Gospel. But the early church didn't create Jesus' teachings!

Or the "Jesus Seminar" (a group of scholars who by voting on which words were actually from Jesus reduced the number of such references to a very few) does not explain the remarkable transforming power of the Gospels. If the teaching content of the Gospels is not from Jesus, then some other source must be found for such profound teaching—what an amazing source that would be! A source as amazing as Jesus?

In dealing with the self-disclosure of God in Jesus of Nazareth, we must include both His earthly life and His exaltation at God's right hand. His earthly life made the revelation of God concrete; made the divine real in the human arena. His Resurrection gives His earthly life its universal meaning, extending the revelation of God across time and the limitations of humanness. This resurrection Christology calls us to the mystery and majesty of worship—to a faith that reaches beyond concepts to an actual identification of freedom and of fellowship.

A liberal view, developed over a century ago by Frederich Schleiermacher, saw Jesus as the Savior in that He had perfect consciousness of God and opens this same possibility to those who follow Him. With modifications, the Mormon Church has a similar view, seeing Jesus as savior in that He shows us the way to participate in deity. I discussed beliefs about Christ at considerable length with Mormon elders during an evangelistic crusade I was privileged to conduct on the steps of the State Capitol building in Salt Lake City in August of 1963. To understand their theology, Jesus is for them a Savior in that He shows them how to achieve a saved future in which they too become divine. Of this system we must ask, where is the Savior who reconciles us with a personal heavenly Father now?

But we should also note other modern interpretations. Several prominent theologians from South America have presented Jesus as the liberator of the powerless. Important insights expressed by Gustav Gutierez and by Jon Sobrino have emphasized that Jesus identified with the problems of injustice and oppression, discovering His identity as the Son of God in achieving God's mission of liberation *(Christology at the Crossroads)*. Similarly black theology emphasizes Jesus as the liberator, finding special identity with the Israelites in bondage to Pharaoh and the acts of God in bringing the people to freedom and equity.

Very significantly, Jurgen Moltmann, a German theologian, gives us a "Theology of Hope" and presents Jesus as "The Crucified God," emphasizing that, in Jesus, God suffered for the salvation of the world. Somewhat more recently, Dennis Ngien, of Toronto, wrote an insightful article in *Christianity Today*, "The God Who Suffers," emphasizing that if God can love, then He must also be able to suffer with us (February 3, 1997). I find this a very helpful presentation, for I believe that God was suffering in and with Jesus on the cross, experiencing the cost of forgiveness at its depth in suffering the ultimate human atrocity (2 Corinthians 5:18-19).

In similar Mennonite identification as mine, Dr. C. Norman Kraus, a theologian and cross-cultural missioner develops what he calls "Christology from a Disciple's Perspective." He examines the dawning of faith on the part of the disciples, expressed by Peter in the words, "You are the Christ" (Mark 8:29). Kraus marks a very important position in emphasizing, "The disciples' faith did not create a resurrection, but the resurrection created the disciples' faith" *(Jesus Christ Our Lord*, Herald Press).

The writings of Dr. Lesslie Newbigin (who has over forty years of leadership as a bishop in the Church of South India) offer significant insights from his interaction with other religions. His lectures, "Christ Our Eternal Contemporary", are one of his earlier contributions (Christian Literature Society, Madras, 1968). In his more recent and more major work, *The Gospel in a Pluralist Society*, (Eerdmans, 1990), he emphasizes interpretation of the Gospel in light of our cultural context. He calls us to have clarity on what is the heart of the gospel so that our conversation with those who do not have faith may provide them with evidence for an authentic faith that they may engage as their own. Here the fact of the Resurrection is unique in Christian witness to persons of other religions.

With the resurrection of Christ, the Scripture is divided into "before" and "after," focused not on stories and precepts about God but on the knowledge of God in Jesus Christ. In our studies we should recognize the relation between revelation (God's self-disclosure), inspiration (the safe-guarding of that disclosure), interpretation (the understanding of that disclosure), and application (the relevance of that disclosure). As we interpret, we recognize that we can never go back and live on the other side of the Incarnation and the Resurrection. The New Testament presents the fulfillment of the Old Testament promises. While building on the Old Testament, it moves from promise to fulfillment. In understanding God's promises, we recognize that Jesus is not a person who was suddenly dropped into history with no credentials, left to make His own claims. He often referred to the fact that His Father was witness to His claims of identity.

To say "All that God revealed *before* Christ, God has then said better *in* Christ" is the nature of divine revelation. This is not to propose a human development of our understanding of God. The divine disclosure is given us in progress through history, until "when the time had fully come, God sent his Son" (Galatians 4:4). Just as a one-dollar bill and a fifty-dollar bill are equally valid tender, yet the one-dollar bill is of less value, so there are preliminary presentations of truth that are not yet of the "Jesus value." For example, in the book of Ecclesiastes, there are some fantastic insights when read in contrast to Greek philosophy of the time. The Hebrew philosopher says that each one of us is personally accountable to a personal God. This is a perspective not clear at all in Greek philosophy. But there are ideas in Ecclesiastes that are inferior to the New Testament. God had more to say and said it best in Jesus. His revelation moves us to a more holistic emphasis on humanness.

In fact, we can say that the treatment of some Old Testament issues is not only pre-Christian but is sub-Christian. Consider the Old Testament teachings on slavery, polygamy, attitude toward women, attitude on war, the practices and extent of capital punishment, etc. The Jesus who taught with authority reinterpreted the Old Testament. He dared to say, "It has been said... but I say unto you," or again regarding Sabbath observance, "The Son of Man is Lord also of the Sabbath," and again, "the Sabbath was made for man and not man for the Sabbath."

The Bible, not being a "flat book," is a grand, inspired, self-disclosure of God that moves from one level to another until reaching its highest expression in Jesus Christ. This understanding enables us to see piety as identification with Christ, discipleship as walking with Christ in the Spirit, ethics as living in the freedom of Christ in love, equity, peace, justice, and mutuality. This understanding sees mission as the calling of the church to be a presence for Christ in all the world, and it means that loving one's neighbor as one's self is to share the gospel with one's neighbor. Wow! What a message, what a word.

Our elementary school education was valid, but we can never go back and live at that level once we have been to high school or college. Just so, we can never go back and live on the other side of the Resurrection. Just as God moved humanity along step-by-step to His full disclosure in Christ, in mission we also help people move on from the limited views of God in their "natural theology" to the full disclosure of God in Jesus Christ.

Again in *The Fabric of Theology*, Richard Lintz writes, "The Reformers held that the proper context for the interpretation of the text is not the subjective interaction between a particular passage and a particular person but rather the interaction of a given passage with the whole of Scripture itself, by its divine origin. And determinations are most effectively accomplished by the corporate study of the Scriptures." The question we should be seeking to answer is not "What does this text say to me?" but "What does this particular biblical text mean, and how does it fit into the entirety of the biblical record?" (pp. 70-73, 93).

In the significant statement from the risen Christ on the Emmaus Road (Luke 24), "He interpreted to them in all the Scriptures, the things concerning himself." This would include the Law, Prophets, and Wisdom literature. He thereby places the Old Testament and the New Covenant in a special relationship that finds its harmony in Him. From this point forward, in the emerging New Testament, we discover a resurrection interpretation guiding us in understanding the Old Testament and giving it new significance.

One approach that helps me in interpreting the whole is to find the basic meaning in a passage; the *principle* for application rather than a "letter literalism." The expression of this principle must take into account the whole of Scripture with its meaning. There are several examples that may help clarify what I mean. As to slavery, the Bible as a whole shows the progress of disclosure correcting this practice until the New Testament maximizes the principle of equity and freedom in the new community. Regarding Sabbath, the teachings of Jesus emphasize the importance of spending time in worship and in fellowship both with God and one another. As to women, the New Testament emphasizes the uniqueness of personhood, gender equality, and mutual respect with diversity of our maleness and femaleness. As to sexuality, the biblical injunctions maximize the meaning of wholeness in male/female relationships, where each is enriched by the other in the oneness of faith, and where passion is transformed by the covenant of love—we are one body.

This approach is a challenge to the contemporary church, a correction for those who see the Bible as a flat plane and thereby justify sub-Christian behavior on the basis of Old Testament passages that are not of the "Jesus character." Their approach becomes much more legalistic, more inclined to a legalistic proof-text approach. It often tends to justify civil religion or approve a militaristic role for Christians, rather than to see our highest loyalty to God who appoints order but who is still "above the powers." Nor can we continue to read the Old Testament primarily as allegory, giving some spiritualistic lessons about one's relation to Jesus, such as saying the story of Joshua conquering Canaan teaches us about conquering enemies that hinder the new life we have in Christ. The conquest of Canaan was in actuality a very "earthy" happening, to be seen as God's establishment of a people through whom the knowledge of Yahweh (Hebrew name for God) would impact the nations and counter their idolatry and worship of tribal deities. Such passages are illustrations of obedience to God, but are not allegories of a "Jesus faith" which people could not yet understand. God's defeat of Israel's enemies was especially a defeat of the enemy's gods, a declaration of Jehovah's sovereignty. The condition of the people determined the nature of God's dealing with them. His judgments were sometimes violent and yet, as with Nineveh, Nebuchednezzar, or Cyrus, He was gracious if people showed a response.

After His Resurrection in the numerous appearances of Jesus to the disciples (Acts 1:1-8), the teaching which He gave them was the same message of the kingdom of God which had been so central in His ministry before the Cross and Resurrection. In this context He also tied himself to the earlier statements of John the Baptist that Jesus would be the One to baptize with the Spirit for He promised to send the Spirit to His disciples. The Gospel is now not only the gospel of the Kingdom but also the gospel of the King! As risen Lord, He has become the Gospel. His victory and exalted person constitute the Good News.

The passage in Matthew 28, commonly called "The Great Commission," is similar in meaning and content as the account in Acts 1:8. We should not read the conclusions of the Gospels as in a sequence moving directly to Acts (1:8 and 2:1-12). Passages like Matthew 28, and John 16 and 20, should be read as the gospel writer's conclusions to his book, statements that parallel the Acts passages. The risen Christ is given "all authority in heaven and on earth" and the exercise of this authority is in being Head of the church—Head of the people of God—and as such He sends us forth as His ambassadors (Matthew 28:19-20, 2 Corinthians 5:20). This charge to mission and evangelism, is directly related to the understanding of Jesus' authority and the extension of His mission in the world (Matthew 20:28).

These passages help us to see that the work of evangelism is not to be regarded as an optional role for a chosen few in the institutional church. The God of reconciliation, at work in and through the reconciling Christ, gives to all His people the ministry and the message of reconciliation (2 Corinthians 5:18-19). This ministry of reconciliation will hold the call to compassion (Matthew 22:37-40), to be in direct relation to the Great Commission (Matthew 28).

A theology that reduces Jesus only to one role—Savior—cuts short the meaning of Christ's teaching and ministry. Jesus, as our Savior, is also the Mediator of reconciliation, the One Lord above all, the Head of the church of which we are functioning parts, the Mentor for our lifestyle, the Liberator in freedom and justice, the caring Shepherd for the needy, the Prince of Peace who calls us to active self-giving love, the Suffering Servant who calls us to service to "the least of these." When we join in solidarity with Jesus, we identify with the whole Jesus. We do not identify only with a select aspect of His work. Paul writes, "We are called to belong to Jesus" (Romans 1:6).

Some persons avoid the impact of the rule of Christ and the authority of His words in the Sermon on the Mount by relegating these teachings to a future time. Such a view sins against Christ and rejects this revelation of the will of God for us now. When His teaching and expected obedience is disregarded as the expression of God's reconciling grace, New Testament teaching is compromised to some humanly designed doctrinal scheme. Paul is misused when it is argued that a Pauline doctrine of justification by faith supersedes the teachings of Jesus as Master. We need to recognize that justification by faith (being saved from sin) is only possible by, and is provided by, the reconciliation brought in Jesus Christ. As Markus Barth says, "This is a justification by the faithfulness of God," or, as I would say, justification by the reconciling God.

In my tradition, the early Anabaptists were orthodox in their acceptance of the Creeds of Nicea and Chalcedon, but they moved away from just following creeds to placing importance on a relationship with the Christ. As a believers' church, we stand in a continuum of Anabaptist faith, hearing the call to discipleship as freedom to walk "in the resurrection of Christ." To concentrate on this core of our faith, we then extend faith as far as possible in life relationships. Such an approach is more effective than to first set boundaries, judging persons as "in" or "out" on the basis of our structures. The covenant of solidarity with Christ will mark out its own boundaries. This calls for a confession of the central teaching of faith, with clarity on doctrine as our interpretation from which we make applications lest we elevate application to the level of dogma itself.

Some make distinctions between "faith-knowledge" and "historical-knowledge," but I am in agreement with Dr. C. Norman Kraus, who says, "We shall begin, therefore, with the acceptance of the New Testament as the reliable witness to the continuity and historical concurrence between the earthly Jesus and the church's experience of the risen Christ" (*Jesus Christ Our Lord*, p. 34). We have no more fundamental basis for faith in the Resurrection than the documents themselves and their claim. I take the documents as the highest authority, the message that Jesus actually arose from the dead.

While in the early phase of working on this manuscript, Dr. Karen Longman, one of the vice presidents at the Christian

College Coalition in Washington D. C., returned from a two-month summer sabbatical in Mongolia. She was leading a group of ten who taught the English language to the schoolteachers of a large region of Mongolia. She relates the rise of a young church, small but vibrant, reaching people for Christ. Most are studying the Scriptures for the first time. She read the gospel of John with a woman who came to believe in the risen Christ and became a newly confessed Christian in the first reading of the Bible. As we talked of this, I began to tease her that these people are coming to Christ without the benefit of the Reformation, Luther, Zwingli, the Anabaptists, and Calvin, I asked her how she could have a Christian faith without conditioning by the theologians that we know. Her answer was of course that this person simply came to Jesus and joined covenant with Him. A primitive Christian fellowship may be possible even in the 21st century!

7

Belonging to the Redeemer

"Blessed be the God and Father of our Lord Jesus Christ! By his great mercy he has given us a new birth into a living hope through the resurrection of Jesus Christ from the dead, and into an inheritance that is imperishable, undefiled, and unfading, kept in heaven for you, who are being protected by the power of God through faith for a salvation ready to be revealed in the last time" (1 Peter 1:2-5).

"But now in Christ Jesus you who once were far off have been brought near by the blood of Christ. For he is our peace; in his flesh he has made both groups into one and has broken down the dividing wall, that is, the hostility between us. He has abolished the law with its commandments and ordinances, that he might create in Himself one new humanity in place of the two, thus making peace, and might reconcile both groups to God in one body through the cross, thus putting to death that hostility through it" (Eph. 2:13-16).

Jesus came not only to make God understandable for us but also to reconcile us with God. Paul sets the cross as the center of his message (1 Corinthians 1). He sees it as the expression of God's self-giving love to the death. He sees the meaning of the

cross as confirmed by the Resurrection and as opening a new
freedom for relationship with God. But we must ask of its meaning as we think from our perspectives as moderns. Was it merely
the death of a martyr or was it the self-giving love of a Savior?
We believe that He is Savior. On the basis of the Gospel and of
the experience of believers for two thousand years, we do affirm
the saving merits of the shed blood of Christ; that is, of His ultimate self-giving to the death.

But how are we assured of this salvation? The answer is that
the Resurrection is God's affirmation of the Cross—of God's
identification with the sacrifice of Calvary. The writer of the
Hebrews says that Jesus, who died on the cross, has now
appeared in the presence of God for us (Hebrews 9:24). His
Resurrection and Ascension become the certification that our
reconciliation with God is made real in grace. As noted earlier,
the Cross is God's self-giving love rather than God acting in
vengeance. God acts in a grace of forgiveness, and this puts us
all on one level as recipients. Paul writes, "God was in Christ
reconciling the world to himself" (2 Corinthians 5:19). He has
redeemed us; we are bought at the price of the death of Christ
on Calvary.

Redemption means that we now belong to the Redeemer!
What a marvelous identity. And this encompasses the whole of
our lives. In Christ, God was acting in amazing self-giving love
to reconcile us to himself. In Christ, we in our humanity are rep-
resented in His humanness. By His identity with us and by His
sacrifice of himself for us, we are being reconciled to God. The
Cross stands as the one authentic and honest meeting place
between God and us. It is the one transforming engagement of
peace and of the creation of a new humanity. Here God is seen
in His total self-giving, and humanness is seen in its total alien-
ation. We are led to repent.

Our assurance of the eternal meaning of the death of Christ
on the cross is grounded in the Resurrection. His was not the

death of an idle dreamer, nor the martyrdom of a great man, but an expression of God's self-giving love to all humanity. Again we note, "delivered for our offenses he was raised for our justification" (Romans 4:25). The last phrase makes clear that the Resurrection provides freedom to walk with God. "God was in Christ, reconciling the world unto himself, and has committed unto us the word of reconciliation" (2 Corinthians 5:19).

The basis for our belief in "Justification by faith" is the work of God in Christ to reconcile us to himself. Justification is in a relationship of faith; it is not something to be claimed apart from identification with Christ. The only person who has the right to speak of justification by faith alone is the one who has left all other loyalties to follow Jesus! As Bonhoeffer has said, "Only he who obeys truly believes, and only he who believes truly obeys" (*The Cost of Discipleship*). This means to believe is to commit, to covenant, and to do so with integrity.

The phrase, "God was in Christ, reconciling..." takes on new meaning when viewed through the Resurrection as God's special confirmation of what happened on the cross. Most theories of the Atonement describe what Jesus did on the cross as His being a go-between in some way appeasing God. But we should rather recognize in the Cross the act of God himself suffering in Christ. The full meaning of the Incarnation will not permit us to think of Jesus only as a go-between, but as the Person in whom God was acting. In a real sense the Cross is God meeting His own demand upon himself in achieving justice. God, too, experiences the pain that is in forgiveness.

Human rebellion calls for correction. It is in the Cross that God's justice engages our rebellion, so that in turn His expression of forgiveness might be just. What an amazing concept of justice, of setting things right, of a transforming dimension of justice in forgiveness. Paul describes this in presenting Christ as the "propitiation" for our rebellion, the expression of mercy that would bring our rebellion to an end. The Cross has become the

Mercy Seat where we meet God, the meeting that changes us, "that he might be just in being the justifier of those who believe in Jesus" (Romans 3:23-26). God's justice is fulfilled in His engaging the cost of forgiveness justly and of being just in accepting us on the moral ground of reconciliation. God in grace is actually setting things right between Him and us. In the freedom of His Resurrection, we are set free.

One of our family's favorite hymns expresses the truth of our faith in this Resurrection power:

> Lift your glad voices in triumph on high,
> For Jesus hath risen, and we shall not die;
> Vain were the terrors that gathered around Him,
> And short the dominion of death and the grave.
> He burst from the fetters of darkness that bound Him,
> Resplendent in glory, to live and to save:
> Loud was the chorus of angels on high,
> The Savior hath risen and we shall not die.
> (Henry Waret, 1817)

Of the many different theories of the Atonement, my own theological reflection has led me to a concept that grows out of the meaning of forgiveness in reconciliation. Reconciliation emphasizes the cost of forgiveness to the One forgiving and focuses on the goal of forgiveness as being life with the risen Lord. I would call this a relational theory, with its emphasis on the Mercy Seat and the work of the Mediator—the one who mediates God's grace to us. Paul says that God was in Christ reconciling the world to himself (2 Corinthians 5:19); and in this sense God in Christ suffered the cost of forgiveness. Jurgen Multmann, in *The Crucified God*, goes to some length to express his conviction that God was present in Christ suffering to forgive. But the goal is reconciliation, to join us to Him in a movement of grace and peace.

The Cross is the expression of God carrying the pain of His own judgment on our rebellion by this act of unqualified love. In Paul's words of the Lord's Supper, he says "whenever you eat this bread and drink this cup, you proclaim the Lord's death (suffering) until he comes," (1 Corinthians 11:26). The Roman Catholic, mathematician/saint, Blaise Pascal, said, "Jesus Christ will be in agony until the end of the age, and we dare not be silent all of that time!" We share with Christ in the freedoms of a new life, of the new creation.

Much modern thought sees Christ's death primarily as exerting moral influence by being an expression of love. But with today's psychological insights we can now grasp more readily the meaning of self-substitution, of the forgiving One who actually substituted himself in the cost of forgiveness. This interpretation does not focus on "punishment" aspects, seeing God as punishing Jesus for us, but on the healing and therapeutic aspects of forgiveness. It is not God punishing Jesus in our place but God in Jesus suffering in our place as the cost of forgiveness. On the other hand, the moral influence theory is weak in that moral influence alone isn't enough to overcome the power of selfish autonomy or individualism. As sinners we would hardly surrender our autonomy simply to follow Christ's "moral influence." Only a profound shift at the heart of our lives, in our psychological nature, can induce the freedom of obedience to His greater personality.

Something happened on the cross that affected God in heaven, fulfilling the expression of His character in divine righteousness, in a love-justice that set things right. And just as surely, something happened on the cross that affected humanity in His "bearing our sins in his body" and, in so doing, opened the way for a love response to grace. This response, this repentance, is a change of our basic attitude toward God. Grace makes possible our response to and our covenant with God. In his nonviolent love we are turned from our violence and self-defense to a partnership of harmony with God. The wonder of it all is that as believers we are now in God's family, and we take on the character of our Father. We are now able to use the familial term of relationship, Abba/Father. In Greek, "Abba" is the term children would use as the name for Daddy or Papa. God is our Father. Even though some may not have had a positive relationship with an earthly father, in Jesus' relationship with God, we now see one who is the ultimate and true Father. Of further note, the point here is not masculinity but a familial relationship.

Esther and I served as speakers at an annual church conference in Montana, and one woman there wrote some striking words in response to the message of the Cross. Speaking of the abuse and deep pain that she had suffered in her life and her new freedom in Christ, she wrote, "Christ will carry the scars of His love forever and so I can willingly carry a few scars while enjoying His forgiveness of my sins."

Both in a "shame culture" and in a "guilt culture" the inner pain of estrangement must be healed. From my observations a "shame culture" is more common amidst polytheistic religions where the social expectations produce shame. A "guilt culture" is more common with monotheistic religions where we are conscious of violating the will of a personal God. The self-giving love of the cross is the dynamic for this inner healing, for the removal of guilt from whatever preconditioning one may have: shame-guilt or moral-guilt.

We must recognize that forgiveness always leads to relationship. It is never merely the experience of release from guilt as an inner experience in isolation from the forgiving One. Thus forgiveness, by its nature, is a reconciliation and calls for careful attention to the meaning of the Cross and the place of "at-one-ment" in Christ. Again, it was God who took the initiative in grace to come to us in Jesus of Nazareth and to make atonement for our sins. The death and resurrection of Jesus changed the relation between God and us. It was a defeat of Satan, sin, and death, but it was not only that. His death and resurrection reconciled us with the heavenly Father. (On reconciliation, see my book *The Robe of God*, chapter 5).

The scandal of the cross—righteous dying for the unrighteous—can only speak of God's involvement in forgiving us. John R. W. Stott quotes P. T. Forsyth, a prominent British theologian of the last century, "Because the holiness of God is meaningless without judgment, the one thing God could not do in the face of human rebellion was to (sit back and) do nothing. He must either inflict punishment or assume it. And he chose the latter course, as honoring the law while saving the guilty" (Stott, *Cross of Christ*, p. 153). He took the punishment himself. This is the profound meaning of self-substitution!

In my theological study and teaching as well as evangelistic preaching, I have for years taught that God the Father suffered at the Cross in/with Jesus, that God as the Son suffered in giving Himself, and God as the Spirit suffered and continues to suffer in coming to work with us by the implications of the cross. In this regard I have mentioned Dennis Ngien's article, "The God Who Suffers" as a significant statement of the meaning of God's acting in Christ to suffer for our salvation (*Christianity Today*, February 3, 1997). I am affirming His emphasis that God's love means His identification with us in such total self-giving that His identity meant suffering to absorb our hostility at a cost to himself.

As I understand the Atonement, I believe that God suffered because of the nature of forgiveness, for the forgiving one carries his own indignation for the sin of the guilty and resolves this indignation in unconditional forgiving grace. And to what depth? The full extent of our sin, of our total rejection of God! God, through the Son, made this forgiveness real in His suffering to the death for us. He became the victim, and forgiveness always begins with the victim (see Miroslav Volf, *Exclusion and Embrace*, Abingdon, 1996).

The wonder of God's amazing grace is expressed in the moving lines of Charles Wesley's hymn:

"Amazing love! How can it be?
That thou, my God, should die for me?"

With Paul, we too, because of the Incarnation, can say that "He who was in very nature God" died for us by becoming in very nature like us (Philippians 2:5-8). According to the letter to the Hebrews, it was necessary for God's Son to die for us on the cross because of the nature of His "covenant." Through His covenant, we are made inheritors, recipients of God's riches (Hebrews 9:15-17). But we can only use this language out of belief in the Trinity. God is not a numerical one but is "One-ness" and the Trinity is not a numerical three but is "Three-ness." The person who died on the cross was not the Father but the Son; the Father was in heaven, yet in a great mysterious way He was there in Christ redeeming us!

We return to the reference from Hebrews where the writer tells us that the crucified Christ has, in the Resurrection, now appeared in the presence of God for us (Hebrews 9:24). This is not just to say that His spirit is alive and well in the other world, but rather that the historic Jesus is risen and is with God. The emphasis shifts from His suffering as sacrifice to His position as our High Priest. His being our risen Lord at God's right hand certifies that God has accepted His redemptive work of death on the cross. In His Resurrection He claims us as His inheritance (Ephesians 1:18); and having led us forth as His own, He has given gifts to us for His service (Ephesians 4:7-12). We are redeemed by His blood—this greatest of all prices. We are His possession. His Resurrection assures that our reconciliation is an accomplished fact.

In Protestantism the focus has been primarily on guilt and the need for justification. His sacrifice has been seen as a means to placate the anger of God. In his book, *Understanding the Atonement*, John Driver says, "In Protestantism the guilt was removed through forensic justification—a legal declaration of righteousness, as if one were already righteous, even though it was not yet the case. In reality, it was a legal fiction (p. 34)." But in Anabaptist theology the focus is on a relation of righteousness, a righteousness in relation to Christ, not a mere declaration of words but an actual reconciliation that brings us into right-relation now. This new relationship removes our guilt, but more, our estrangement, our rebellion, our being prodigals, our enthronement of self-will in the place of God's will. But in redemption it is the heavenly Father who has in Christ come to us in grace. God made the sacrifice. This is the expression of grace, and it isn't cheap!

There is a remarkable sequel to the story of the Passover deliverance in the book of Exodus, to be found in the story of God claiming ownership of the first-born and trading them for the Levities who would be His priests (Numbers 3). God, having spared the first-born, had a claim of ownership on them and would demonstrate this in the trade for the Levites. The exchange was to count the Levites, 22,000, and then to count the firstborn and there were 22,273. They then made the trade, but since there were more first-born sons than there were Levities, God sold the 273 first-born to Israel and the money was placed in the treasury (Numbers 3:40-48). In this story we see that redemption was not *from* whom, but rather *to* whom; they were redeemed to be God's possession. Paul picks this up in the words, "You are not your own; you have been bought at a price. Therefore honor God with your body" (1 Corinthians 6:19-20). To be redeemed means that we belong to the Redeemer!

In my judgment, this adds a dimension to the "Christus Victor" perspective, in that while Christ is victor over Satan, sin, and death, His atoning death on the cross not only liberated us from the demonic but also *primarily ransomed us to be God's own possession*. We are redeemed to belong to the Redeemer; we belong to God, we are children of God, and in this resurrected fellowship we are free. The confrontation with Satan at the Cross was an "in-your-face" confrontation with evil, a victory that confronted the evil and drained it of its power. But Jesus was victor on the cross, *through* the Cross, for in death He experienced all that violence could do and remained free, "that by the grace of God he might taste death for everyone" (Hebrews 2:9).

Redemption liberates us by making us free as God's children. While being God's Son, Jesus as the Incarnate Christ is not ashamed to call us brothers and sisters, His own faith-siblings (Hebrews 2:11)! We are members of the family of God. As John writes explicitly, "Behold what manner of love the Father has bestowed on us, that we should be called the children of God! And that is what we are" (1 John 3:1). The victory of the Resurrection makes this new life-relationship to be a reality for us as disciples. We have a life of freedom in Christ, freedom to walk with Him, freedom from the tyranny of sin, freedom to look up and say "Abba, Father!"

His Resurrection confirmed and announced the victory of the Cross and before the hosts of heaven and the legions of hell the risen Christ is seen as victor (1 Peter 3:18-19). The evil principalities and powers have been "unmasked," that is, shown for what they are, and defeated— put under His feet (Colossians 2:15). This exposure, by Christ's love on the cross, has limited the power of Satan, and he is not to "deceive the nations" any longer. The mission of the church is to keep announcing this fact. And the victory of Christ is firmly established in the Resurrection. With the Cross shown to be the cost of forgiving love, the Resurrection extends that love forever. The forgiving Cross and the transforming Resurrection constitute the Gospel of our Savior and our Lord. As James Denney points out, there is "no salvation from sin unless there is a living Savior" (*Death of Christ*, p. 73).

As we have examined the claim of Christ's divine sonship we should further note the ground of forgiveness as expressed by

Peter in his first sermon on the new order, saying, "God raised him from the dead." Peter and the apostles affirm, "Salvation is found in no one else, for there is no other name under heaven given to men by which we must be saved" (Acts 2:24, 4:12). Grief has given way to astonished joy: "He is risen." Indeed it is good news. The Gospel has come to humankind as the action of God in grace. There is one name, and no longer need we search through a maze of religions to find peace with God. Salvation is not by our religious works but is by our response to God, the most wonderful God thinkable, a God of amazing self-giving grace who cares more about us than about himself. This is a God who purposes to win us rather than a God to whom we must win access. What good news!

This Gospel of the Cross becomes the heart of Paul's message, for in his word at Thessalonica, and in his message in Athens at the Areopagus, "Paul was preaching the good news about Jesus and the resurrection. God has given proof of this to all men by raising Jesus from the dead" (Acts 17:1-3, 31). In his defense and in his messages he couples his faith in our future resurrection with the resurrection of Christ. As the "first begotten" from the dead, Christ is the first of many multitudes who will be resurrected (Acts 24:15, 21; and 26:8, 23).

Sharing with a group who traveled to Calcutta, India, to attend the Mennonite World Conference, January 1997, we visited some of the great sites in India: New Delhi, Agra, and the Taj Mahal, then to Varanasi and the Ganges River which is so sacred to Hinduism. We went on to Bhod Guya where Buddha received his enlightenment, but in each setting there was no evidence of joy or peace. As we were in boats on the Ganges, observing all of the oblations, the funeral pyres, and exercises of religious rites at the edge of the river, I stood in one of the boats and read the passage in Acts 17 of Paul's address at Mars Hill where he speaks of the many gods celebrated by the Greeks. How rich and meaningful the words of that passage, in the

Indian setting of altars representing the 33 million gods of Hinduism, focusing on the marvelous message of the resurrection of Christ. The Christian's assurance and joy is faith in the risen Lord who reconciles us to God. How wonderful the singularity and the simplicity of the Gospel with its focus on Jesus as "the way, the truth, and the life."

In a striking statement regarding the full reconciliation we have with God, Paul says, "Christ is made the end of the law for righteousness." That is, Christ is the end of regarding the law as a way to rightness with God, for now we see Christ as the One in whom we enter right relation with God (Romans 10:4). As risen Lord, at God's right hand, He negotiates as our advocate, He as our "partner" represents us before the Father just as the Holy Spirit is His "partner" here with us.

Just as we in the Christian tradition must put our faith in the God of grace who saves us at the cost to himself expressed in Christ, so members of other world religions similarly cannot be saved by faith in their system of religion but must reach out by faith to the God of grace of whom their religion can only be a searching thought. In our exercises of Christian faith we must be clear in pointing beyond our own rites of religion to the fact that salvation is only in covenant relation with Christ. Our honesty about this fact, including our own systems of doctrine, will help persons in other religions to look beyond their religious rites to God himself—the God we know in the person and grace of Christ. The biblical emphasis on salvation by grace is a call to recognize the otherness and the mystery of God as well as a recognition that our salvation is not by any achievement through *our* goodness but through *His* goodness. We share this Gospel of grace so that all peoples alike may come to God by faith, may know a faith made clear in Christ.

After declaring the place of the death and resurrection of Christ as the heart of the Gospel, (1 Corinthians 15:1-11), Paul presents a clear statement on the relationship of the

Resurrection to the authentication of our salvation (verses 12-22). In the first chapter of Ephesians, Paul gives us one of the most wonderful presentations of God's purpose in Christ and the achievement of that purpose in the Cross and Resurrection; the extension of His "incomparably great power for us who believe. That power is like the working of his mighty strength, which he exerted in Christ when he raised him from the dead and seated him at his right hand in the heavenly realms, far above all rule and authority, power and dominion, and every title that can be given, not only in the present age but also in the one to come" (Ephesians 1:19-21. This is similarly expressed in Colossians 1:20-23).

The writer of Hebrews contrasts the victory and the position of Christ our Mediator with the work of Moses as a mediator of God's will to His people. The point made is that Moses was faithful "in" his house, but Jesus is faithful "over" His house, emphasizing the better covenant brought by Jesus the new Mediator (Hebrews 8:6, 9:11-15). The call to covenant fidelity is expressed in descriptive words: "Therefore, since we have confidence to enter the Most Holy Place by the blood of Jesus, by a new and living way opened for us through the curtain, that is, his body, and since we have a great priest over the house of God, let us draw near to God with a sincere heart in full assurance of faith, having our hearts sprinkled to cleanse us from a guilty conscience and having our bodies washed with pure water. Let us hold unswervingly to the hope we profess, for he who promised is faithful" (Hebrews 10:19-23).

The writer of Hebrews also relates the resurrection of Christ to the continuing role of His being our one high priest, the One who ministers to God on our behalf. "Because Jesus lives forever he has a permanent priesthood. Therefore he is able to save completely those who come to God through him, because he always lives to intercede for them" (Hebrews 7:24-25). He is there, at God's right hand, as the eternal certification that God has acted consistently with His justice in correcting the problem of human estrangement, but at a cost to himself. This is one of the central images of the work of reconciliation, negotiated by the high priest through Israel's history but now expressed in its ultimate meaning in Jesus. He is the "priest forever, in the order of Melchizedek" (Hebrews 7:17), that is, one appointed by God other than from the Levitical order. He is God's appointee by grace.

Our experience of the Cross is personal, not theoretical. We come to the Cross to experience salvation, to give interpretive dimension to our faith, to enjoy assurance in faith. We should understand as much as possible the reasons for the Atonement. The work of H. E. W. Turner, in *The Meaning of the Cross*, helped me to find a place for what to me is a biblically consistent interpretation, a view with the emphasis on reconciliation. God initiates a new relationship with humanity by taking the burden of His own wrath upon himself—and substituting himself in total sacrifice. He becomes truly human in Jesus, judges humanity in himself and provides triumph over evil and death by the divine act of raising Him from the grave. Therefore Christ is the reconciler who takes away sin and condemnation from human persons. Because Christ does this, He is also the victor over all powers and authorities. He is the one Victor, the one Redeemer, and the one full expression of God's self-giving love.

This emphasis, interpreting the Atonement from the perspective of reconciliation, I have called a "relational" or "personal" understanding. The Cross is an essential element of forgiveness and relationship, for the cost of forgiveness is God substituting himself for us in Christ. As J. Denny Weaver writes, the Cross is God's suffering in nonviolence the violence of humanity with a love that brings violence to an end (*The Nonviolent Atonement*). The sacrifice is God's self-giving; it is not made by Christ in separation from the Father but an expression of love in which God is involved in a total self-giving sacrifice.

From my theological perspective, there is an importance in emphasizing both God's forgiving grace and also God's transforming grace. Holiness is wholeness, our belonging wholly to God and being made whole in Him. The Cross reconciles us to God, for in the Cross God is reconciling us to himself, and through the Cross, He continues to separate us from sin. As Christ's disciples, we share the resurrection freedom; we are on the victory side of the Cross! We are to live in this victory and when temptations come we declare this victory afresh, affirming, "I still mean it," standing by faith in Christ (Romans 6:11).

In Christ our rebellion against God is brought to an end. Our estrangement has been corrected; we are now in a right relationship with God (Philippians 3:9). The freedom we know in Christ is freedom from the rule of a depraved nature, not from its fact. We are changed as an act of God in inner transformation, creating us as new beings by sharing in the resurrection life and the Spirit's indwelling in our life.

Release from the dominance of depravity is by the superior power of the Divine Presence. This is not a righteousness of works, it is not a claim to perfection, but it is an actual right-relatedness with God to be enjoyed with assurance and peace. While depravity is our condition it is not our confession! We are reconciled in grace. In humble recognition of the mystery of the Cross, we accept it as God's act to engage humanity in a divine grace of reconciliation. Here is the one ground on which we come to God with the honesty which confesses our violence against God, and it is the one ground on which God meets us all alike in His forgiving grace.

8

Christ-Centered Ethics

"So if you have been raised with Christ, seek the things that are above, where Christ is seated on the right hand of God. Set your mind on things above, not on earthly things. For you died, and your life is now hidden with Christ in God. When Christ, who is your life, appears, then you will appear with him in glory. Put to death, therefore, whatever in you is earthly seeing that you have stripped off the old self with its practices and have clothed yourselves with the new self, which is being renewed in knowledge according to the image of its Creator. In that renewal there is no longer Greek and Jew, circumcised and uncircumcised, barbarian, Scythian, slave and free. Yet whatever gains I had, these I have come to regard as loss because of Christ. More than that, I regard everything as loss because of the surpassing value of knowing Christ Jesus my Lord. For his sake I have suffered the loss of all things, and I regard them as rubbish, in order that I may gain Christ and be found in him, not having a righteousness of my own that comes from the law, but one that comes through faith in Christ, the righteousness from God based on faith. I want to know Christ and the power of His Resurrection and the sharing of his sufferings by becoming like him in his death, if somehow I may attain the resurrection from the dead" (Philippians 3:7-11).

On September 11, 2001, my memory went back to the fall of 1981, living in Washington, D.C., when I was invited to come to the Pentagon and to speak in a chapel. On that occasion as I walked down the hall a man met me and asked, "You are a Mennonite, a pacifist. What has a Mennonite to say in the Pentagon?" I said, "Come and see." As I addressed the audience I spoke from Luke 6, Jesus' sermon in which He calls us to love our enemies, to turn the other cheek, and to go the second mile. I emphasized this as the Christian's strategy of operation, not the way of a wimp. This strategy is not the surrender of a weakling, but says that we don't have to treat others as they treat us. We are free to choose our own action by our own principles. This is the lifestyle of the kingdom member. Further, if we would use this approach toward those we call enemies, we could relate on a different basis than the one on which they act.

After my message those military men came by in a line to shake my hand and tell me that, while they were not pacifists as I was, they respected what I had said and wanted to find better ways to work for peace. This is, in my understanding of Jesus, the calling for His disciples to act out of the freedom that we know in Christ. While we do not expect government to live and operate by the ideals which are voluntarily accepted by those who walk as Christ's disciples, there are values in the teachings of Jesus which can enrich the lives of even humanists who will read Him openly and honestly. And, in a remarkable turn in our history, President Regan negotiated a change of relations with the Russians.

When I speak of discipleship, it is discipleship in grace, walking in the freedom and fellowship of Christ. Speaking of Christian ethics must be a focus on ethics in grace. What does that mean? How do we relate salvation by grace and ethical responsibility? Earlier I said we should relate ethics to Christ in the same way in which we relate salvation to Christ. We are saved by relationship with Christ, and we live out our relationship with Christ. Note again Paul's words, "It is for freedom that Christ has set us free" (Galatians 5:1).

This perspective on a liberating relationship in grace, in my thinking, expresses the biblical view. The Anabaptist concern for ethics was set in the context of a discipleship in grace showing that a relationship with Christ is essentially free from legalism. The Resurrection ethic is not an obedience based on merit but an "obedience of faith" (Romans 1:5, 6:16).

Paul places the preaching of the Cross and Resurrection at the center of the Gospel. The Cross is effective because the crucified One lives. His power is extended in all time, but this is an extension of His suffering love. We who follow Him live by the same nonviolent love. I have frequently shared a story told of the novelist Alexander Solzhenytsyn, when he was in the Soviet Gulag as a prisoner. Caught in the despondency of hopelessness, he dropped his shovel, went over to an old bench and sat down with his head in his hands, expecting the guard to pick up his shovel and crack his head open and it would all be over. Suddenly he felt a presence, and looking through his fingers he saw an old man sitting by his side with a stick in his hand. Extending the stick he placed it between Solzenytsyns' feet and drew a cross in the dirt. Without a word he got up and walked away. Solzenytzyn sat there looking at the cross and suddenly all of the truth of God's self-giving love rested upon his heart and he was transformed. He got up and picked up his shovel and went back to work. Little did he realize then that God would bring him out of there and use him as a voice to the world for justice and righteousness.

We have seen the Resurrection to be the certification of Jesus' relationship with the Father and confirmation of the victory of His Cross. In a similar way the Resurrection confirms the authority of Jesus' teachings and their validity for the life of His church. The risen Jesus is the same Jesus, and His message continues to carry the meaning for the believer today that it did when given. The Sermon on the Mount, along with the marvelous teachings of John 12-17 and other passages, outlines both the spirit and the lifestyle for the disciple of Christ. The life and ministry of Jesus is the expression of the will of God, of the norm for Christian living and our norm for ethics.

It is important that we do not see Christian ethics as a new law—as a simple set of rules—but as freedom in the love of Christ. Ethics begins for the disciple with the implications of our pledge to follow Christ. We have noted Paul's statement, "If you are risen with Christ, seek the things that are above, set your affection on things above and not on things on the earth" (Colossians 3:1-2). Similarly, Paul states that we being baptized into Christ are baptized into His death, and are risen with Him to walk in newness of life (Romans 6:1-6). The implications of this 'new life' of freedom point us to a Christian lifestyle, to a dynamic and transformed walk with Christ. We can live each day in fellowship with our risen Lord Jesus.

Ethics usually refers to one's standards of conduct and morals. In my theology, ethics is simply the expression of Christian discipleship. In fact, discipleship may be spoken of as *applied ethics.* It is the ethic of freedom in Christ, of the new creation, of a style of life in freedom and love as we walk with Jesus in the way. As I have noted, it is specifically what David Bosch called "A Spirituality of the Road." It is recognizing John's meaning, "Whoever says, 'I abide in him,' ought to walk just as he walked" (1 John 2:6). It is an ethic of liberty, the freedom to live "in Christ" and to walk with Christ.

This ethic enables us to celebrate the richness of life. The story is told of a geography class in which the teacher was discussing the Seven Wonders of the World, with several lists including one each for the ancient world, the modern world and of the natural order. She asked the class to compile a list and she then asked them to share their candidates. Receiving the most votes were: Egypt's Great Pyramids, the Taj Mahal, the

Grand Canyon, the Panama Canal, the Empire State Building, St. Peter's Basilica and China's Great Wall. While gathering the votes the teacher noticed one student, a quiet little girl, who hadn't turned in her paper and asked her if she was having trouble. The quiet girl said, "Yes, a little. I couldn't make up my mind because there are so many." The teacher said, "Well, tell us what you have and we may be of help." The girl hesitated, and then began to read, "I think the Seven Wonders of the World are: to touch, to taste, to see, to hear—she hesitated a bit, then added—to feel, to laugh and to love."

Ethics for all of us finds its expression in human values, but, in the community of the redeemed, ethics finds its character especially in the person of the Redeemer. Our behavior is not determined by rationalizations about our fallen-ness or sinful inclination to self-centeredness, but is determined by our new life in Christ. We are called to be God's, predestined to be conformed to the image of His Son (Romans 8:29). This is God's purpose for us and it is possible as we share in the victory of His Resurrection. Paul is best understood through his belief in the Resurrection, for, like us, his relationship with Jesus was a relationship of faith, not sight. Unlike the earliest disciples, who walked with Jesus in His earthly pilgrimage, Paul had only a relationship with the risen Christ. And yet, as with his contemporary apostles, (the original disciples), after the resurrection of Jesus they were just like Paul and walked with the risen Lord. And so it is with us. We love the One whom we have not seen but believing we relate to Him in life.

We must not read Paul in separation from the Gospels with their accounts of the life of Jesus. For example, Luke, as Paul's contemporary, similarly had not been one of the twelve disciples. In his research Luke came to know about Jesus quite thoroughly but his relationship, as was Paul's, was a relationship with the risen Christ. This is the same Jesus who is now known in His Resurrection and yet the same historical Jesus in whom we have the substance of the self-disclosure of God. "he is the image of the invisible God" (Colossians 1:15). With Paul we must say, "I want to know Christ, and the power of his Resurrection, and the fellowship of his sufferings, becoming like him in his death" (Philippians 3:9).

In the risen Lord we are relating to the One who is "the same Jesus" who lived and taught in Galilee, who died and rose again in Judea. I want to make this my highest quest, to know Christ in ever increasing intimacy and integrity.

As we look at the character of the new life in Christ we discover that this liberating love is an extension of the love Christ expressed in His life and death, and which He now expresses in and through us. Disciples of Christ are participants in His love and being so loved are changed into persons who express love. Such practices of love are the disciple's strategy of operation, both in mutual relationships and when faced with hostility. Again, as Jesus said, "If someone strikes you on one cheek turn to him the other also" (Luke 6:29); love of this kind is not surrender. In fact it is the strategy of reconciliation. This is the life of a witness, for it says in essence "Your treatment of me does not determine my treatment of you."

In addressing this strategy of love, I must affirm again, that in the freedom of treating others as we would have them treat us, we have a principle that is not only for personal relationships, but when taken seriously by a nation, it can change our relations with other countries of the world. We should treat others as we would be treated, taking the positive approach rather than reacting to what others do and responding in their style.

The strategy of love is a freedom that in itself gives the disciple of Christ a psychological advantage. When you turn the other cheek, when you go the second mile, it is such a departure from the usual that the opponent will often ask, "What makes this person different?" We are free to decide on the basis of our identification with Christ how we are to respond to the other rather than to have our response determined by the other's action toward us. We are not passive. We decide a course of action by the principles of Christ and guidance of the Spirit. In this freedom we confront the other with evidence of the reality of the kingdom of Christ.

Many of us remember the stirring words of Martin Luther King Jr. during the Civil Rights Movement; "Our ability to absorb suffering will out-wear your ability to inflict it." Or again, "We must not only avoid violence of deed but violence of spirit." Again, "Darkness cannot drive out darkness, it takes light to do that; and hate cannot drive out hate, it takes love to do that." Our participation in the Resurrection enables us to live by a principle of grace that is higher than the normal reactions of our sinful inclinations. If understood, this becomes the dynamic for social change, for the transformation of human relations this is far more potent than any use of force or violence.

The risen Jesus Christ asked Peter the question each of us must answer: "Do you love me?" The ethic of the disciple is the liberating power of love! It begins in grace as God establishes a liberating relationship between himself and us. The ethic of love then creates a liberating relationship between us and others, providing unity with diversity. It also creates a freedom for the disciple in the world by giving us a calling or mission; we are liberated from becoming enslaved to some lesser cause.

In Peter's conversation with the risen Christ, he is called to a new ethic of love—first, in his own relation with the Lord, and, secondly, as he takes his place among his fellow disciples. Particularly, Jesus gave him something to live by in the new community, an ethic of liberating love toward God and toward our fellows. Plus, when Peter made reference to John, Jesus essentially told Peter to trust God to determine the other person's role (John 21:20-22).

Further, our ethic as disciples is Christocentric—grouping all things around Christ. It is important to recognize that such a

Christocentric ethic is not, on the one hand, simply an attempt to copy or to live by the Sermon on the Mount as though in a new legalism, nor on the other hand does it mean that we need not live by the Sermon on the Mount or by Jesus' other teachings. Rather we join in solidarity with Jesus. We identify spiritually with the Teacher himself. From this identity we will seek to express the character of His life and in this expression we will seek to conform our lives to the pattern of His teachings including the Sermon on the Mount. This ethic is our new relationship with Christ.

In Paul's epistles the language of identity is often expressed by the phrase "in Christ," a phrase which speaks of our relationship with Christ. Again, in a particularly personal way, Paul wrote to the Romans, "Therefore I urge you brothers and sisters, in view of God's mercy, to offer your bodies as living sacrifices, holy and pleasing to God. This is your spiritual act of worship. Do not conform any longer to the pattern of this world, but be transformed by the renewing of your mind. Then you will be able to test and approve what God's will is—his good, pleasing and perfect will" (Romans 12:1-2).

The disciple's commitment is to participate in God's grace and calling, a calling to holiness and love (Ephesians 1:4-5), to peace and justice in our relationships. This is not a commitment to a code but to solidarity with the person of Christ, a fellowship with Jesus that results in a Christ-like life. Ethics, for the disciple of Christ, is a matter of spirit before it becomes a matter of behavior.

As followers of Christ, we seek to serve others rather than to dominate them. We regard persons of various races, especially other than our own, as a gift of God and an enrichment of our social life. We regard the poor and needy as opportunities to extend our sense of community and to express our love. We use money in the service of Christ rather than for status or power. Jesus' call to love and peace is more than a rejection of violence toward others, it is a call to shalom, and to the wholeness and well-being that God would extend to all. To quote Mother Teresa again, "We will be judged by treating Christ in the way we have treated the poor."

Jesus began His "be-attitudes" by saying, "Blessed are the poor in spirit, for theirs is the kingdom of heaven" (Matthew 5:3), and again, "Blessed are the peacemakers, for they shall be called the children of God" (Matthew 5:9). Martin Luther King Jr., in his prophetic words to his people said, "We must beware of violence of spirit as well as violence of deeds." Those of us who are disciples of Christ are called to take literally Jesus' call to be peacemakers. To live by such love and compassion rather than by self-defense and the exercise of power, will be both humbling and demanding.

Having Christ as a basis for this new lifestyle is expressed by Peter in his emphasis on the example of Christ. "To this you were called, because Christ suffered for you, leaving you an example, that you should follow in his steps."

♦ He committed no sin, and no deceit was found in His mouth *(holiness)*.
♦ When they hurled their insults at Him, He did not retaliate *(nonresistance)*.
♦ When He suffered, He made no threats *(humility)*.
♦ Instead He entrusted himself to Him who judges justly *(faith)*.

"He himself bore our sins in his body on the tree, so that we might die to sins and live for righteousness; by his wounds you have been healed. For you were like sheep going astray, but now you have returned to the Shepherd and Overseer of your souls" (1 Peter 2:21-25).

There is a dynamic and creative aspect of righteousness that is to be expressed as an ethic of mutual respect. This was seen in Jesus' comments to Peter about his relationship with his colleague John. Each situation we face calls us to a creative response designed to encourage the other person's trust in Christ. This relationship is one of righteousness, of right relation or a refusal to misuse another.

While this is not the approach of "situation ethics," it is an approach that achieves "situational relevance." We are committed to walk with Christ in life and to live out His love in our social relationships, whatever the situation. We come to each situation with the constant of our relationship with the risen Christ, with the dynamic of His shared agape, and with the reality of His model as our touchstone. But as we come with the love of Christ we need to make creative applications that can bring into play resurrection power in a clear expression of our Christian faith and values. In the actual life context in which we live and work, a creative application calls for the discernment of the Spirit, both through the Word and through the redeemed community.

The very clear thrust of the eighth chapter of Romans is that of walking in the Spirit. In it Paul describes the child of God as one that "does not live according to the sinful nature but according to the Spirit" (Romans 8:4). This means that we do not live selfishly, do not manipulate others for our own interests. For us and for others, this is an ethic of right relationship, a spirituality of freedom. The key is in his statement, "If the Spirit of him who raised Jesus from the dead is living in you, he who raised Christ from the dead will also give life to your mortal bodies through his Spirit who lives in you" (Romans 8:11). This is a call to live at a level above the pursuits of selfishness. It corresponds to his earlier statement, "Sin shall not be your master, because you are not under law, but under grace" (Romans 6:14). Of this change he writes, "But thanks be to God that, although you used to be slaves to sin, you wholeheartedly obeyed the form of teaching to which you were entrusted. You have been set free from sin and have become slaves to righteousness" (Romans 6:17-18).

Practical advice on how to live as disciples of Christ is found spread throughout the Epistles but most often in the concluding chapters of the letter after the writer has laid the theological foundation for the application. This is especially clear in the "encouragement" section of Ephesians: chapters four, five and six. In his letter to the Philippians the tone is somewhat different, with an emphasis on "working out in life's expression what God is working into our experience" (Philippians 2:12-13). A further emphasis is focused on the righteousness (right relatedness with God) that comes from God by faith in Christ (Philippians 3:9-10). In Colossians there is a rich passage on prayer for a spiritually informed and empowered understanding of God's will for daily living (Colossians 1:9-12), and a call to live in fidelity, integrity and holiness (Colossians 1:22, 2:6-10, & 13-22). I have found the writings of my friend, Dallas Willard, *The Spiritual Disciplines,* to be very helpful in application of biblical truth to personal life.

An ethic of the new creature liberates us from self-centeredness. It liberates us in our being members of the family of God to now be brothers and sisters in a community of grace. It liberates us in the world to be on the offensive for Christ rather than on the defensive, as His ambassadors of reconciliation. The only free person in society is the person who is non-conformed to the world, who turns the other cheek, and who does not have behavior toward others determined by reaction to that person's behavior. In Christ we are free to live by His agape—His love. This love, as expressed uniquely in Christ, will also be extended through us as disciples of Christ. We are called to live not in our own strength but in the limitless power of the Resurrection.

In the letter to the Hebrews, the writer gives us a beautiful resurrection-centered benediction, but it is at the same time a call to righteous living: "May the God of peace, who through the blood of the eternal covenant brought back from the dead our Lord Jesus, that great Shepherd of the sheep, equip you with everything good for doing his will, and may he work in us what is pleasing to him, through Jesus Christ, to whom be glory for ever and ever. Amen" (Hebrews 13:20-21).

9

The Privilege of
a Priestly Lifestyle

"You are a chosen race, a royal priesthood, a holy nation, God's own people" (1 Peter 2:9).

"To him who loves us and freed us from our sins by his blood, and made us to be a kingdom of priests serving his God and Father, to him be glory and dominion forever and ever. Amen" (Revelations 1:5-6).

"For he is our peace; in his flesh he has made both groups into one and has broken down the dividing wall, that is, the hostility between us. He has abolished the law with its commandments and ordinances, that he might create in himself one new humanity in place of the two, thus making peace, and might reconcile both groups to God in one body through the cross, thus putting to death that hostility through it. So he came and proclaimed peace to you who were far off and peace to those who were near; for through him both of us have access in one Spirit to the Father. So then you are no longer strangers and aliens, but you are citizens with the saints and also members of the household of God, built upon the foundation of the apostles and prophets, with Christ Jesus himself as the corner stone. In him the whole

structure is joined together and grows into a holy temple in the Lord; and in whom you also are built together spiritually into a dwelling place for God" (Ephesians 2:14-22).

One of the greater principles of the Reformation is "The Universal Priesthood of the Believer." This, in comparison with the old covenant, or Old Testament, is a new freedom in the body of Christ. This is a dynamic not only of coming to God directly for one's self but of being engaged in priestly service for others. Being a priest at another's elbow is a fantastic privilege—to walk with another into the presence of God—what a remarkable participation in faith! Christian faith is not individualistic but is participation with others, bridging differences and witnessing to the new order God is creating.

Out of the horrible tragedy of September 11, 2001, the terrorist evil, there were many remarkable stories of compassion and faith. There was a new spirit in America of togetherness, that we suffered together and that we could support one another. Being a priest at another's side took on more immediate meaning, crossing racial, ethnic and religious lines.

In 1966 I was privileged to share in the Congress on World Evangelism that met in Berlin. On one occasion a few of us were chatting together in the rotunda of the Congress Hall. Suddenly a Palestinian brother, Anis Sharosh, came through the door to our right and started walking across the rotunda. At the same time a Jewish brother from Israel came through a door to our left and was crossing the room. The two men encountered one another and as they met they paused. Suddenly we heard the one man say, "I saw my people killed by your people." The other man responded with similar intensity, "And I saw my people killed by your people." The atmosphere was charged, intense. Suddenly the two men reached out their arms, smiled, embraced and we heard one say, "Isn't it wonderful to know a Christ who makes us brothers!" This is the new dynamic of a priestly relationship.

The social changes the Gospel brings are in the reconciliation of different peoples. We have a new community in Christ, a redeemed people in the freedom of grace. This is Christ's primary work in the world, creating a people for Himself that will make the kingdom a reality. This is a new people from all nations, Jew and Gentile, the hidden mystery of God's purpose before the foundation of the world (Ephesians 3:1-6). And we are called to be participants in this revolutionary social change, to actually be priests of God. What a wonderful privilege to be called into His new order, a fellowship that transcends racism, ethnicity and prejudice by the unity of the Spirit, an order in which we are each a priest at our brother's/sister's elbow. It is this priestly lifestyle that creates a spiritual community rather than a cultural or ethnic assembly.

The church is not to be thought of primarily as an institution but as redeemed people. It is a people who are called to belong to Jesus and as such into a fellowship, a koinonea, which gathers in His presence. The risen Christ is present with us, and we walk into God's presence with Him. His church is "a habitation of God by the Spirit" (Ephesians 2:22). Above all, Christ promised that where several gather in His name He is present (Matthew 18:20). He calls forth believers as persons who identify with Him and become a part of His body. He, as exalted Lord, is given to be head of the church and He mediates His presence to us through the gift of the Holy Spirit. As John writes, Christ "lives in us by his Spirit which he has given to us" (1 John 3:24). We are now given the priestly function of coming into God's presence together.

In our day the concept of church has become so institutional that persons miss the relational part of community—even of meaningful conversation with other believers. In our discussions we dialogue over issues rather than to engage conversation as fellowship. The term "Christian" has been reduced to the designation of a religious movement rather than to mark the quality of a disciplined faith. To be a Christian should be understood as a person who is identified with Christ. It may be helpful, since the word Christianity is so institutionalized, if instead of referring to ourselves as Christians, we would speak of being followers of Jesus. God's intent is to call a people in His Name, to create a fellowship of people under the Lordship of Christ, to extend His kingdom through persons walking in discipleship with Christ. Our beliefs about Christ and the meaning of His Resurrection mean that we as believers are in solidarity with the risen Lord, in communion with Him, and as such our community with one another is actually a priestly function of bringing one another to God.

The new order indicates a spiritual oneness that is created by our common relationship with Christ. It is not simply an ethnic, or denominational, or a sociological relationship. Rather it is a people who are one with our Lord as spoken of in His prayer in John 17, a people, who in oneness of spirit, honor His Spirit. As head of the church, as Lord of this people of faith, He enables and energizes the new people of God to be His priestly presence in society. He is the Savior of the body and we, as diverse parts, complement one another in the function of this body. We are bound together by the presence of the Spirit.

The early church confessed the Lordship of Christ, and in this confession, they emphasized the deity of Christ as the Son of God. As Wolfgang Pannenburg says, "This was the use of the Kyrios title for the exalted Jesus" (p. 265). The Kyrios is the risen and exalted Jesus whose return we await as His community but whose presence we celebrate as we gather to worship. The Aramaic petition for the presence of the Lord at the Eucharist, "Maranatha," meaning, "Lord come" (1 Corinthians 16:22), is an expression of this faith in the reality of presence. This shows one aspect of the faith of the early church—expecting Christ's presence in their worship. Church happens, community is a gift of grace; church is experienced wherever persons confess together that Jesus is Lord! Some persons talk of how a people "do church," a term which seems too functional to me and is not relational in meaning. In His grace we are being the church. By His presence it is happening to us. To meet in His name is to exercise our priesthood as believers.

In the passage from Ephesians opening this chapter, the victory of the Cross is shown as interrelating the redemptive and the ethical, Paul writes that "He has made of two, one new humanity, so making peace...for through Him we both have access to the Father by one Spirit...being built together to become a dwelling in which God lives by his Spirit" (Ephesians 2:14, 18, 22). This is the greatest social change conceivable, making of Jew and Gentile a new unified humanity! And this is the nature of the community of Jesus, a new unified humanity. We are participants in a totally new order, living by a new covenant, an actual community of the kingdom living as "resident aliens" in the world (see *Resident Aliens,* by Willimon and Hauerwaus). This has political implications for the believer. There is one Imperial mandate, one Lord, and His kingdom has priority in our decisions for belief and behavior.

This new commonality is created in Jesus, by Jesus, and around Jesus—the risen Jesus. As Dietrich Bonhoeffer has said, "Community means that we relate to each other through Christ, not directly" (*Life Together*). That is, there is more to our relationship as persons in Christ than the human social element. If we should relate to another directly, we may well be guilty of intimidating, manipulating, dominating, or coercing the other, but when we relate in and through Christ, we are both free while yet being in covenant. In this way we may minister to one another and for one another as priests by one another's side.

Again, His purpose in redemption is the creation of a new order as a people of God. We are redeemed, that is, we belong to Him, and we are His possession. As Paul wrote to the Galatians: "It is for freedom that Christ has made us free"

(Galatians 5:1). Further, this community of the redeemed is a colony of heaven on earth (Philippians 3:21). True, we live in a fallen world, but we who are redeemed do not live by the desires of our fallen nature, we live by the freedom and qualities of the new life we are given as redeemed in Christ. As I have stated, to be fallen is our condition, but it is not our confession! His church is people who in naming His name join in solidarity with Him. His church is trans-cultural, trans-racial, and transnational. His church is the expression of the global networking of His kingdom, the redeemed walking in faithfulness to the Redeemer.

In the small but global denomination of which I am a part, a million plus several hundred thousand, this is demonstrated in many ministries around the world. Programs such as Mennonite Economic Development Associates have enabled business and professional persons to be enablers of others in various cultures of limited development. The Mennonite Central Committee programs of relief and service have placed persons as "agents of reconciliation" in difficult settings, including African countries in turmoil, Ireland with its violence and the Balkans in its repeated wars. Other groups are doing similar work, as expressed for example by World Vision. In being there as a presence for Christ, Christian brothers and sisters serve as priestly expressions of the peace and justice to which we are called in Christ's kingdom. When we relate to each other as a people in Christ, we are not imposing a western culture on others but rather sharing the character and quality of God's new order in every culture.

Culture itself is neutral but always tends toward idolatry. Christians are not trying to develop a Christian culture as such, but trying to be the church within culture—in the world but not of the world. We engage or mix with the culture as our vehicle of living but are free in it to live out the life of Christ. Today, especially with the need for a peoplehood that includes the diversity of races, we should add a perspective to deal with racism between the white and black communities.

In emphasizing a relational ethic, I stand with Dr. Cheryl Sanders of Howard Divinity School that "Christ is the bridge between cultures." Cultures are vehicles for broadening the human experience. The Spirit of Christ brings compassion, acceptance, and an understanding of differences to the life of this new people. We have found that the church in the urban context is relevant only as the several peoples are made a new unified humanity—one community of the Spirit. As evangelical churches we have not done well at this, but by God's grace we must!

This is especially relevant for us in relation to the problems of the Middle East. We of the Western world need to learn how to be our brother's brother, refuse to regard our Arab neighbors as second-class citizens, avoid using our power to drive others into a corner or to keep them from saving face. We should be pro-Israel only in the same spirit and degree to which we are pro-Palestinian (note Isaiah 19:19-25). If we could hold our government responsible to do as much in the area of financial aid to the Palestinians as we do for the Israelis, we would see a major change in the Middle East. In fact, greater equity could correct the motivation in such cultures for youth to join a terrorist cause. It is important that we model and call our opponents to join us in seeking equity, justice, and peace for all peoples and to work together for a better global society for our children and grand-children. Ours should be a mission of peace for the good of all peoples and with the awareness that nonviolence and peace is our only security for the future.

The nature of spirituality in this new priestly order is another continuing challenge in renewal. This has become a quest that crosses the lines of distinction in the Christian community, and between various religions. In the Anabaptist tradition, spiritual-ity is usually thought of as discipleship, which includes worship, prayer, praise, fellowship, integrity, witness, and service. In emphasizing discipleship, we must recognize the privilege of our priestly role in relation to one another. We must also take seriously the cost of these disciplines, look at the strengths, and consider the danger should we become legalistic. The cost of discipleship is in actually recognizing Jesus as Lord and sharing His cross in life. Jesus said, "If any one will come after me, let him deny himself, and take up his cross daily and follow me" (Luke 9:23). The strength of discipleship is that in our being linked with Jesus as risen Lord we receive His Holy Spirit and are transformed, empowered, and gifted to live the Christ life. Its danger is that we tend so readily to structure, codify, and create a legalism of constraint out of our discipleship.

With our understanding of Christian experience we should focus on the new life in Christ rather than simply focus on forgiving of sin. Salvation is far more than dealing with our guilt—as important as this may be. It involves a walk with the risen Christ in love. But we must take seriously the inner experience and the outer expression, the inner reality and the external behavior. The inner love for God and the outer love of neighbor must be held together. This, however, is not an obedience to law but a freedom in the Spirit to practice love. As one of my 16th century mentors, Michael Sattler, has written, "There are two kinds of obedience—the outer, servile obedience and the inner obedience of the Spirit of Christ" (Yoder, *The Legacy of Sattler*).

In looking at spirituality we think of Origen and Clement and Gregory of Nyssa and of such mystics as John of the Cross and Teresa of Avila. Thomas Merton, a Trappist monk of the Cistercian tradition, has been an outstanding proponent of "image mysticism" in the spiritual life during the 20th century. John of the Cross, in *Spiritual Canticle, Living Flame of Love,* and in *The Dark Night,* calls us to union with God. He calls us to a transformation, which he sees to be much like that of a log of wood when placed in the fire. Not to minimize the values of this emphasis, the priestly lifestyle is larger and less inclined to a 'private piety.' The Resurrection and the fellowship in the Spirit call us to be totally transformed with as much emphasis on the ethical as on the emotional dimensions of union (see Dupree, et al pp. 80-90). It is not just burning for God but behaving with God that expresses our spiritual walk.

The Christian church since the Reformation has had major stress on being pronounced right with God and minor stress on holy or right living with God. The biblical understanding of the victorious life in Christ, of the power of the Spirit to counteract evil and to live in the will of God, has been too little understood. We talk of being new creatures but we fail to concentrate on how a new creature conducts life! Yet Paul writes in his letter to the Colossians, "Since then you have been raised with Christ, set your heart on things above, where Christ is seated on the right hand of God. Set your minds on things above, not on earthly things. For you died, and your life is now hidden with Christ in God" (Colossians 3:1-3). In this passage Paul goes further in describing the break with the old life and calls us to the continuing action of faith in putting off anything inconsistent with the new life. This shows us the character of the redeemed community.

In the epistle of Romans, Paul expresses the character of this sanctified life. "We died to sin; how can we live in it any longer? Or don't you know that all of us who were baptized into Christ Jesus were baptized into his death? We were therefore buried with Him through baptism into death in order that just as Christ was raised from the dead through the glory of the Father, we too may live a new life" (Romans 6:2-4). Paul does not say that sin is dead to us. Sin is a very constant possibility. Rather he says that we have died to sin; our response pattern is totally changed.

This new life, "walking in newness of life," is what the *Schleitheim Confession of 1527* puts in focus, saying that "baptism is for those who will walk in the resurrection of Christ." Baptism is not simply a break from the old life but is a covenant in which we share and live in the new life. In his remarkable book,

A Spirituality of the Road, the late Dr. David Bosch, a Reformed theologian of South Africa, calls for practicing faith as bearing the cross in tension with the secular world (Herald Press, 1979). He expressed this at a time when the situation of apartheid made the possibilities of a social change without violence seem impossible. But he called the church to follow the way of love and thereby to find freedom from revenge. Today we recognize the miracle of South African opposition leader, Nelson Mandela, coming out of twenty-seven years in political prison and eventually serving as President of this country with no sign of a spirit of revenge.

A significant story relating to Mandela's release emphasizes this freedom. Bill Clinton was then Governor of Arkansas and was watching TV the evening Nelson Mandela was released from prison. He quickly called his wife and daughter to watch what he told them was a historic event. He noticed as Mandela walked out the gate and looked at the people gathered there, anger flushed his face and then it disappeared. Years later, when Clinton was President of the U.S. and Mandela was president of South Africa, the two men met. Clinton asked him about this, that he had seen the anger but had never seen it since. "Yes," Mandela responded, "You are right. When I was in prison the son of one of the guards started a Bible class I attended and I met the Christ. That day when I stepped out the gate and saw the people gathered there suddenly I felt angry at being robbed of twenty-seven years of my life. But then the Spirit said, "Nelson, while you were in prison you were free, now that you are free don't become their prisoner."

Freedom is an inner matter. For us to understand the character of freedom in our new priesthood in the victory of Christ, we should look carefully at Romans 6:6: "For we know that our old self was crucified with him, so that the body of sin might be done away with, that we should no longer be the slaves of sin." (In the Greek, done away with is the word 'katargeo,' meaning devitalized.) Some forms of theology have made a mistake in figuring out the meaning of this text, assuming that the old self, or "old man" is synonymous with what is called in the next phrase "the body of sin." This assumption has led some to say that in the crucifixion of the old self we got rid of the body of sin and our potential for sin. Others equate the two and hold that since we still have the sin potential we are still "packing the old self around." The former have a pseudo claim to perfection, a claim that often leaves persons defeated by the awareness that they are not so free. The latter tend to excuse their lack of holiness by the assertion that they are continually struggling with the "old man."

A correct interpretation clarifies that we are released from the old self as the realm of life in which sin reigned. This means that the body of sin or aspect of self that is inclined to sin by seeking its own way has now lost its power to dominate or to control one's life. The new self lives under the Lordship of Christ, and as such we can have a priestly function in relationships.

Similarly, John writes in his first epistle that since we have been born of the Spirit we can now say "no" to sin. We are released from the practice of sin; we no longer live in rebellion. One might even read John's words "can not sin" as meaning, we "can now say no to sin" and its temptations (1 John 3:9). The victorious life is not the removal of or the denial of sinfulness in our make-up. It is the wonderful, positive, affirmation that we have a new life, a superior presence, an ability to say "no" to the prompting to sin and the available power to make this commitment stick. This is living in the power of the Resurrection! We are spiritually energized. This is being energized by the power that raised Christ from the dead (Romans 8:11).

Another remarkable passage in this regard is in Paul's letter to the Galatians. "So I say, live by the Spirit, and you will not gratify the desires of the sinful nature. For the sinful nature desires (present tense in the Greek, meaning continually desires) what is contrary to the Spirit, and the Spirit desires (present tense meaning continually desires) what is contrary to the sinful nature. These are in conflict with each other, so that you do not do what you want" (subjunctive form expressing something that is conditional in the Greek), we do not do what we would if the Spirit was absent! (Galatians 5:16-17). This speaks of the surpassing greatness of His power in us for victorious living. By the Spirit's presence we do not behave in the way we would have behaved in the absence of the Spirit.

The interpretation of this passage from Galatians 5 may be illustrated by recognizing sinfulness as something like the pull of gravity. Hold a book out in your hand, the pull of gravity is constantly there pulling it down; but since your hand is constantly there lifting and overcoming the pull of gravity, the book cannot fall because you have it, you overcome the pull of gravity. Just so, the Spirit in us is a counter-acting presence, a power to keep us from being self-centered, helping us overcome even our inclination to sin. This is the work of the risen Christ within us through His Spirit, a work to secure us in His will so that we can be His priests to one another.

The story is told that in a little church in Croatia there was an altar boy named Josef Brose assisting the priest in the mass. He fumbled the glass cruet and dropped it on the floor. The priest was angered and struck him on the face, whispering loudly, "Get out, get out, and don't come back." The altar boy left and never came back; he grew up to be Tito, the Marxist leader who was a cause of suffering for so many people.

But at the same time in Peoria, Illinois, there was an altar boy by the name of Peter John assisting Bishop Spalding at morning mass, and he made a similar mistake and dropped the glass cruet on the floor. Years later he wrote, "You can't imagine the sound of a glass cruet breaking on a cathedral floor, it seemed louder than an atomic explosion." But this priest looked at him, smiled, and whispered, "Someday you will be standing where I am."

This boy grew up to become known as Bishop Fulton J. Sheen, a name taken from his mother, and was used of God in his radio program, in his written books, and by his television ministry to bless hundreds of thousands.

What power and influence in the spirit of our relationships, the tone and words with which we share. The words of Paul about the fruit of the Spirit are basically attitudinal, a fruit that brings us to a new freedom.

The priestly life is lived before the Lord and is a life of freedom rather than a life of turmoil within one's being. When one is surrendered to Christ, the nature of the conflict changes to "conversation" between options. We walk in the freedom of Christ, recognizing the temptations and tendencies to go our own way but exercising the faith walk of identity with Him.

In numerous passages it is emphasized that the new order Christ is building is a community of the Spirit. In the first references to the development of the Church, the risen Christ promised the disciples that they would be baptized with the Spirit in a few days (Acts 1:5-8). As we move through the book of Acts we meet Resurrection Christians who are the result of the creative acts of the Holy Spirit. It is His presence that creates the community of God's people (Acts 3:26; 19:5-10; 20:20, 24-25). Peter sees the Resurrection as having "given us a new birth into a living hope," the work of the Spirit extending the victory of Christ in us (1 Peter 1:3-5, 10-12).

Paul's statement about the essential nature of the new humanity is unique; "He himself is our peace, who has made the two one, to create in himself one new humanity out of the two, thus making peace." And to this Paul adds, "Through him we both have access to the Father by one Spirit...and in him you too are being built together to become a dwelling in which God lives by his Spirit" (Ephesians 2:14, 15, 18, 22). As redeemed people, we are not simply a religious association, but a fellowship in oneness with Christ, by the presence of His Spirit. This is a community of the reconciled, and a community of reconcilers! We are priests to one another, His agents of reconciliation (2 Corinthians 5:18). This reconciliation crosses all racial, cultural, tribal, and national lines. We become one new people of God composed of many peoples.

Today, with hundreds of denominations, imperfect as they are, they are interpretations of various expressions of the work of the Spirit. We must refuse to idolize any denomination—including our own. The church should be consciously multi-denominational, respecting and learning from different expressions of the Spirit in history.

In the midst of increased urbanization, pluralism, and international association we need to discover the dynamic of community, which I have been addressing. I do not mean simply a social togetherness but a relationship enabling one another to be responsible disciples of Christ. Small groups within congregations can become enriching modules of larger communities so that congregations will be enriched by them as an association of the reconciled.

Congregations are enriched by the sub-communities of covenant groups or koinonia groups that involve persons in more intimate sharing of faith and vision. These groups can be for the enriching of the congregation without being congregations within the congregation. This has been our experience in the inner-city congregation where I was the pastor at Washington Community Fellowship on Capitol Hill, in Washington, D. C.

To clarify the pattern the congregation developed as charter members, we composed a membership covenant which made it possible for persons to become full members of the congregation and yet retain their various denominational affiliations. That is, they could join our church to be Mennonite with the sponsoring denomination, or they could join and remain Presbyterian, Baptist, Methodist, Evangelical Free, etc. This unity in Christ with diversity became a stimulus for the whole congregation to center our faith on Jesus, our quest being to know Him better. The emphasis was on the core of faith more than on the boundaries. This resulted in a very alive, diverse, stimulating congregation, quite deeply united in spirit, fellowship, and mission.

At the Lusanne, World Congress on Evangelism, in 1974, I heard Canon Michael Green of the Church of England say, "We need to rediscover that the church itself is a part of the kerygma." (Kerygma is Greek for the essence of the Gospel.) That is to say, it is good news in a broken, fragmented, hostile world to discover there are actually communities of love, fellowship, justice, and peace to which they can turn. Such communities will be evangelistic by the very nature of their expression of being a caring people, for their very presence in society will beckon others to God. It is then that the words of Emil Brunner will find fulfillment, "The church exists by mission as fire exists by burning."

The risen Lord identifies closely with His church in the world. When Saul had his Damascus Road conversion, Jesus did not ask why Saul was persecuting the church, but rather, "Saul, Saul, why do you persecute Me?" (Acts 9:4). Jesus had said earlier in reference to his judgment at the end of the age, "In as much as you have done it unto one of the least of these, my brothers you have done it unto me" (Matthew 25:31-46). In practicing His love we are His brothers! In His church we love God and in doing so love the neighbor. Jesus, in the story of the Good Samaritan, told the lawyer the question is not, "Who is my neighbor?" but rather "Are we willing to be neighbor?" The example and spirit of Mother Teresa has become a universal symbol in her conviction that you show your love for Jesus in your love for the poor and powerless. What a remarkable example of this truth.

The risen Christ has bound himself to the church until the end of the age. Jesus said, "All authority is given me on heaven and on earth, and lo, I am with you always, even unto the end of the age" (Matthew 28:20). What an affirmation of His "valuing" us, His people, His kingdom in process! The church is His investment, He has given His life for us, and He identifies with us as His most important work. Paul speaks of "His inheritance in the saints" (Ephesians 1:20).

The late Ralph Buckwalter, a Mennonite missionary in Japan for most of his life, expressed this meaningfully in a devotional poem in his journaling.

"I saw Jesus today
in my brother friend.
He could have defended his views
with skillful debate.
But quietly,
Calmly
He waited...
And spoke the right word.

I saw Jesus today
in my brother friend.
He could have done it all himself
with vigor
But patiently,
Kindly,
He shared...
And delegated responsibility.

I saw Jesus today
in my brother friend.
He could have laid them low
with a single blow.

But humbly,
Patiently,
He forgave...
And waited on the Lord.

I saw Jesus today
in my brother friend.
He could have split the church
with his (self) righteous cause
But prayerfully
Graciously
he stooped...
And washed his brother's feet."
(Ralph Buckwalter)

10

Our Hope
in Christ's Return

"I do not want you to be uninformed, brothers and sisters, about those who have died, so that you may not grieve as others do who have no hope. For since we believe that Jesus died and rose again, even so, through Jesus, God will bring with him those who have died. For this we declare to you by the word of the Lord, that we who are alive, who are left until the coming of the Lord, will by no means precede those who have died. For the Lord himself, with a cry of command, with the archangel's call and with the sound of God's trumpet, will descend from heaven, and the dead in Christ will rise first. Then we who are alive, who are left, will be caught up in the clouds together with them to meet the Lord in the air; and so we will be with the Lord forever. Therefore encourage one another with these words" (1 Thessalonians 4:13-18).

There is freedom and joy in knowing that Jesus, our Sovereign, is coming to earth again. He is yet to complete the kingdom, which He has introduced. As members of His kingdom we are in the world but not of the world. Our citizenship is in heaven, and we live now as participants in the eternal order. We are strangers and pilgrims here, looking for that city whose builder and maker is God. In days of increased violence, increased poverty and social need, this promise becomes, as Paul says, "a comfort" (1 Thessalonians 4:18). The apostle Peter writes, "Seeing then that all these things shall pass away, what manner of persons ought we to be in all holiness and godliness" in our order of life (2 Peter 3:11). We are a people of freedom, a people who can order our lives as members of the kingdom of God.

Jesus' victory will yet be disclosed in a totality, a completion still to be expressed. This He has promised us and in this hope we live. He is returning to bring to consummation the full meaning of redemption! This is our hope, our assurance, and our security. Just as the Resurrection demonstrated that God's purpose did not end with Christ's death, so His promise points us beyond our own lives to the greater realities of life in His triumphal return. It is the resurrected Christ who promised that He would come again. This hope enables us to live in freedom and in grace.

This perspective adds dimension to the believer's life and in this sense Christian hope is a dynamic for meaningful living. A person without a future has no meaningful life in the present. Hope for the future is to one's spirit what oxygen is to the physical being. Without hope, without a sense of future, one's life suffocates. A resurrection Christology gives us that hope, both for meaning in the present and for an unlimited future. Hope is an extension of faith into the future. Hope is not mere wishful thinking but assurance that God will fulfill His promises.

During the C. S. Lewis Centennial at Oxford, England, in which Esther and I were sharing, I heard Dr. Michael Cassidy of South Africa, relate the work of the church to overcome apartheid. He told of speaking out for equity and justice in his radio ministry, and he was called before the President of the country. He was ordered to cease such expressions and his ministry of social transformation in and through the church. Undaunted he turned to his colleagues and said with a gesture toward the President, "If anything happens to me you will know the source of what happened." He continued his work and at one time over 35,000 persons gathered in a stadium in prayer for an end to apartheid in South Africa. This is one illustration of the "already" of the kingdom.

The Gospel of Christ is the Gospel of His grace and glory, including the glory of His kingdom. This kingdom has both the dimensions of the "already" and of the "not yet." We come to Christ now to know salvation in His reconciling grace. We have the assurance that He has accepted us and that He transforms us in His grace. Paul writes that God has "translated us from the kingdom of darkness into the kingdom of the Son He loves" (Colossians 2:13). This is the "already." And yet the full realization of the glory of His reign is yet before us, the "not yet." To live eschatologically means to live with the assurance that the future has already begun in our lives as we move toward the "telos," toward the consummation of all God has promised.

Our focus on the future, on His return, helps us to order our lives in His will. John writes of this hope, "And everyone who has this hope set on him purifies himself" (1 John 3:3). Dr. Leslie Newbigin tells of reading in the journal of Scott's expedition to the South Pole, that at one point the expanse of white snow and the horizon were so completely merged that they could not keep from going in circles and stumbling on their own tracks. Finally they made snowballs and threw them ahead of them so that they could follow this direction and walk in a straight line and thereby find their way (*Christ Our Eternal Contemporary*, p. 37).

Our future includes the certainty that the risen Christ will return. He promised this to His disciples and it is confirmed by the Holy Spirit in the writings of the New Testament. Someone has counted that His "Parousia" or return, is spoken of some

168 The Resurrection Life

three hundred times in the New Testament. In the Revelation of
Jesus Christ, we hear the words, "I am the Alpha and the
Omega," says the Lord, "who is, and who was, and who is to
come, the Almighty" (Revelation 1:8). Again in the same chapter we read, "I am the First and the Last. I am the Living One.
I was dead, and behold I am alive forever and ever! And I hold
the keys of death and hades" (1:18-20). For the believer, this fills
us with great expectation.

This story, from the funeral service for Dr. Samuel Proctor,
the well-known, highly-esteemed black preacher of New York
City, was shared with me. At the memorial service numerous
persons were asked to share tributes and the service got longer
and longer. Dr. Beecher Hicks, distinguished black minister of
Washington D. C. was the final speaker, but the group preceding him moved one after the other until finally coming to Jessie
Jackson with his rather lengthy presentation. Now it was
Beecher Hickes' turn and the audience was restless and he knew
that his time needed to be short. In his inimitable style, he
stepped to the desk, looked off in the far corner of the ceiling
and called out, "Sam! Sam! Sam! Just wait there by the door; I'll
be coming along soon and we'll go together to the feet of Jesus
and offer our praise." And with this he sat down. The audience
was mesmerized and will long remember the personal and
meaningful expression of those words.

In the account of Christ's ascension, the message of the
angels was that "in like manner as you have seen him go into
heaven, he will come again" (Acts 1:11). Each time that we celebrate the Lord's Supper we show forth the Lord's death with the
words "until he comes" (1 Corinthians 11:26). In the first
covenant celebration, we remember that Jesus sat at table with
His disciples and said of the bread, "This is my body," and of
the cup, "This is my blood of the covenant which is poured out
for many," to which He added that He would not drink this
again with His disciples until drinking it in His kingdom

(Mark 14:22-24). It is with this perspective that Paul writes "as often as we eat this bread and drink this cup we do show forth the Lord's death *until he comes*" (1 Corinthians 11:26). I remember seeing the last part of this phrase on the front of the communion table when preaching in the large Baptist church in Walnut Creek, California—"Until He Comes." It is a phrase that helps to keep our hope in focus. We live in the hope of His return and this hope is a transforming dynamic in our lives; "Until He comes."

There is a remarkable account of Karl Barth, a titan of twentieth century theology, who on the evening of December 9, 1968, telephoned his godson, Ubuck Barth, and quoted a hymn that speaks of Christian hope. Later that evening, he and Eduard Thurneysen, a friend for 60 years, chatted by telephone as they often did, recalling that in their lifetime they had been through two global wars, the Nazi period and the darkness of the world. Then in parting Barth said, "But keep your chin up. Never mind," and added in the words of their fellow countryman, Christoph Blumhardt, "He reigns!" That night Barth died in his sleep. This is our affirmation as well—"Jesus reigns."

But to live in the hope of the return of Christ and the ultimate fullness of His reign is not to overlook the fact that as Sovereign Lord at the right hand of God His reign is already being extended in and through those who acknowledge Him as Lord. Dr. James McClendon speaks to the present meaning of our hope in his review of the "Seven Articles" of the *Schleitheim Confession*. He sees in the creation of this Reformation statement a clear sense of eschatology already breaking in—by the ethics of resurrection—with "an emphasis on resurrection walk to which they were committed" (p. 271). The word "Vereinigung," translated "union," or reconciliation, gives evidence that the conferees have been reconciled to Jesus Christ and the Confession sets forth a simple structure for church order, understood as a way of life. McClendon adds, "Ethically, this structure of Schleitheim set the conditions for the free church and, if (Ernst) Troeltsch is right about the larger scene, it was determinative for the later Free State and the Bill of Rights as well" (p. 271).

While our sense of eschatology emphasizes a present reality that in some degree is realized in the kingdom of grace, there is yet more to enjoy in the coming kingdom of glory. Included with our hope of Christ's return is our belief in the resurrection of the dead, and in our own resurrection with the victory of those who "sleep in Jesus" or "rest in Jesus" as accompanying Him in His triumphal return. His Resurrection is the assurance of our resurrection. Our certainty that He lives is the basis of our hope. As Wolfgang Pannenburg says, "The reality of the resurrection of Jesus is definitively and irrefutably decided only in connection with the eschatological resurrection of the dead...with all the implications that the Easter message is true" (p. 331).

As we look specifically at eschatology, or understanding of the end times, there are primarily four ways to interpret the Biblical eschatological teaching. First is the idealist, or symbolic interpretation that takes away the time aspects of the apocalyptic and regards the symbols as timeless truths not tied to any particular time. Second is the futurist interpretation, held in some form by many of us, which sees these prophetic elements, related directly to an "end time" when they will all come to pass. Third, there is the historicist interpretation that sees the writer speaking of events which were at that time yet future but which are being worked out in the life span of the people of God or the church. And fourth, there is the preterist approach—the "last times" have arrived as the Scripture writers described them. We have the Old Testament statements about these events pointing to a future but in the New Testament the last days have now come.

A Christological approach would suggest that in Christ the future has come and is being brought to actuality in His kingdom, both in aspects already and also in aspects that are "not yet." This we refer to as the kingdom of grace and the kingdom of glory. This approach emphasizes the futurist interpretation. (See Millard Erickson, *Contemporary Options in Eschatoloty,* for discussion of Bultmann on "Existential Eschatology" and Moltmann on "Theology of Hope" pp. 35-51.)

A striking reference to the meaning of Christ's work as risen Lord is the calling forth of His kingdom, its present creation, and its future completion. In possibly his most significant passage on resurrection, Paul writes, as we have noted earlier, that when Jesus has completed His kingdom He will "deliver the kingdom over to the Father" (1 Corinthians 15:24). This is a very clear statement expressing the "already" of building a kingdom and moving to its completion.

In his letter to the Romans, Paul speaks of the implications of this telos or finishing act for the created order, "that the creation itself will be liberated from the bondage of decay and brought into the glorious freedom of the children of God" (Romans 8:21, see verses 18-25). It is significant that in the earliest epistle Paul wrote, the first letter to the Thessalonians, in every chapter there is a reference to the return of Christ and consummation of His work. We are to live with this faith.

Peter speaks of Christ's return in his challenge to the religious leaders who objected to and who criticized the disciples' interpretation of the healing of the crippled man at the gate of the temple, affirming this in the name of Christ (Acts, chapter 3). Note Peter's words, "Repent, then, and turn to God, so that your sins may be wiped out, that times of refreshing may come from the Lord, and that he may send the Christ who has been appointed for you—even Jesus. He must remain in heaven until the time comes for God to restore everything as he promised long ago through his holy prophets" (Acts 3:19-20). This statement that He will correct what has been perverted by sin includes the fact that God has a future for this created world. This adds a theological perspective that calls us to be stewards of creation, for us to engage special concerns about ecology (Romans 8:20-24).

In Paul's letter to the Ephesians, he says that it will take the ages of the ages for God to unfold to us the riches of His grace (Ephesians 2:7). That is a long time—the ages of the ages! God has a lot planned for the future. Our lives should be set in the context of the eternal. We live and serve in light of this larger relationship, that of the eternal purpose of God. Paul says to us, "you shine like stars in the universe as you hold out the word of life—in order that I may boast on the day of Christ that I did not run or labor for nothing," (Philippians 2:15b-16). He speaks to Christians then and now, of our responsibility but also our accountability to the Lord. We live in harmony with His purpose and we serve in harmony with His pattern and expectation.

To speak of His return is to speak of the "telos," the climax, the end or culmination of history. This telos will be the achievement of the full and final aspects of God's redemptive work. History does not determine its own destiny nor contain its own fulfillment. God is sovereign and He will bring about its fulfillment. And this "reality" is not only for those of us who may be alive when He returns but for the Church triumphant which is made up of all those who "have fallen asleep in Jesus." These He will bring with Him when He returns (1 Thessalonians 4:13-18). We may be sure this includes all of our loved ones who have preceded us in death and who have lived and died by faith in Christ! The *Apostle's Creed* says of His return, "He will judge the quick and the dead."

When loved ones die, we sorrow but our sorrow is not as that of those who have no hope in a resurrection life with the Lord. A few years ago my father was terminally ill. I visited him those last weeks, driving several hours from Washington, D.C. On my last visit a few days before he died, I left him saying the German word for farewell, "Aufwiedersehn," a word meaning "I'll see you again!" This is our hope and our faith, believing deeply in the promise of God and being able to say, "I'll see you again."

One of the essential aspects of a "resurrection Christology" is trust for our own resurrection. Jesus said, "I am the resurrection and the life. He who believes in me will live, even though he dies, and whoever lives and believes in me will never die" (John 11:25-26). In a very significant theological insight, Pannenburg relates resurrection and creation, to say that Resurrection means the Creator will create new form for us: "Paul puts the resurrection of the dead alongside of creation out of nothing. The Easter event and the resurrection on which Christian hope is set are no less limitless than creation. Only the Creator can awaken the dead, and resurrection from the dead shows what it means to be Creator. Resurrection is the supreme enactment of the will of the Creator that wills the existence of creatures" (p. 417).

Paul wrote one of the most pointed passages on the relationship of the resurrection of Christ to our future resurrection in his letter to the Corinthians (1 Corinthians 15:24-58). In this passage he relates the reality of the resurrection of Christ in a changed but an actual body to the expectation and assurance of our resurrection in a different but actual bodily form. I do not know what this form will be like other than to draw from the references to the appearances of the risen Christ, but even His resurrected form was different in various expressions than was His pre-death physical nature with its limitations.

The Judaic/Christian concept of resurrection, affirmed by Job and David but interpreted by Jesus, is related to the whole concept that as humans we are "unitary beings." We do not speak of living on as immortal souls in the Greek concept of immortality, but we recognize in the immortality, which "Jesus brought to light," that we are immortal *persons* (2 Timothy 1:10). Jesus spoke of actual persons being present in the future kingdom, of "sitting down with Abraham, Isaac, and Jacob in the kingdom of heaven" (Matthew 8:11). Further, He added, "God is not the God of the dead but of the living," giving us one of His clearest words on resurrection reality (Matthew 22:32).

This is a far more profound reality than the limited, if not puny, idea of reincarnation as a recycling of the soul. Yet such thought is proposed by many out of the instinctive feeling that life is too meaningful to end. As stated earlier, the philosopher Emmanuel Kant had this inner sense that life is too valuable for it to be completed in a mere seventy or so years; hence he held that we must be immortal.

Our hope of resurrection is built on the fact that Christ himself arose. He is spoken of as "the first fruits" from the dead. His Resurrection guarantees ours. This is more than simply affirming the immortality of the soul as an extension of existence for the intellect or spirit. The Easter event shows us the actual resurrection of the person. As He lives, so we will live again in the presence of God, to be with Jesus our Lord for the ages to come. This is a strong incentive for holy living. John writes of our hope in Jesus' coming as a motivation for holy living: "When he appears we shall be like him, for we shall see him as he is. Everyone who has this hope in him purifies himself, just as he is pure" (1 John 3:2-3).

Our faith in the future resurrection is an expression of our belief that Jesus is alive, that He is risen, that He is at God's right hand, King of kings and Lord of lords. And in contemporary music we sing:

> "Majesty, worship his majesty,
> Unto Jesus be all glory, honor and praise,
> Majesty, worship his majesty,
> Jesus who died, now glorified, King of all kings."

The picture in Revelation of the risen Christ is given in many symbolic forms. One of the most poignant is of the sacrificial lamb of the Old Testament. The symbol is used in praise to

Him in identity with "God who sits on the throne and to the Lamb" (Revelation 7:10). This vision into heaven is further described in poetic or hymnodic form showing our relation to the Lord by redemption through His blood. Speaking of the many believers in heaven, we read:

> "These are they who have come out of the great
> tribulation,
> They have washed their robes
> And made them white in the blood of the Lamb.
> Therefore, they are before the throne of God,
> And serve Him day and night in his temple;
> And he who sits on the throne will
> Spread his tent over them.
> Never again will they hunger;
> Never again will they thirst.
> The sun will not beat upon them,
> Nor any scorching heat.
> For the Lamb at the center of the throne
> Will be their Shepherd;
> He will lead them to springs of living water.
> And God will wipe away every tear from their eyes"
> (Revelation 7:14-17).

The book of the Revelation is actually a presentation of how things look behind our life scenes. Oscar Cullmann has emphasized what he calls "Heilsgeschichte," salvation history, to express the perspective of God's work in redemption through history. This means that beyond history as sequence of events there is history as divine purpose. The book of the Revelation presents the work of the risen Christ, present in the midst of the church now (chapter 1), but acting as Sovereign Lord as the ages unfold.

Vernard Eller has read the Revelation as a tract for nonresistant martyrdom (in *The Most Revealing Book of the Bible*). The saints, as followers of the Lamb, are not depicted as warriors in martial violence, but are witnesses to the death, who follow the example of Jesus, and who overcome the evil "by the blood of the Lamb" (Revelation 12:11). While the saints celebrate with the Lamb, the presentation of Armageddon or a final climactic battle does not show His followers participating in martial violence. He, the Lamb, overcomes the evil powers (Revelation 19-20), and does so with the sword of His mouth, His word. Eller says the millennium celebration is for the fulfillment of the martyrs whose lives were cut off because of their identification with Christ in a hostile society.

In study of the book of Revelation, I concur with those who believe that it is a presentation of Christ in His full victory, as the Cross and Resurrection present Him as "Christus Victor." In the book of the Revelation, the writer is showing us the victory of the Resurrection, the Lordship of the risen Jesus, as over against the power and violence of the Roman Empire. The church is to be free in its nonviolent spirit in the midst of suffering and the violence expressed against the church. The rule of God, the reality of the kingdom, is presented with great and meaningful symbolism.

I offer a suggested outline from my personal study of the book of Revelation. It seems to me that following the first chapters there are three major divisions of the main part of the book. The first three chapters serve as both introduction and preparation for the extended discussion. In chapter 1 we have the remarkable picture of the risen Christ present among the churches, especially relevant for the church today. This is to "tell it as it is," that Christ is present in/among His church. Then in chapters 2 and 3 we have the revealing presentations of Christ as Lord confronting and holding the seven churches accountable. These challenges are equally relevant for today's church.

Following this introduction, I see three major divisions of the main body of the book of the Revelation. In something of a presentation like the art of the Sistine Chapel, one picture following another, we are given a survey of God's purpose in history.

The first major section speaks of the **"Triumph of God's Program in Time,"** (chapters 4-10). Much of the material in chapters five through seven, and the opening of the seven seals, can be related directly to the sequence of Emperors from Tiberius and following, but with applications for the church today.

The second section deals with the **"Triumph of God's Power Over Evil"** (chapters 11-18). J. Nelson Kraybill, in *"Imperial Cult and Commerce in John's Apocalypse"* (AMBS), along with other writers, shows the economic, commercial, and social exploitations of evil and the righteous judgments of God.

And the third section is the **"Triumph of God's Purpose Beyond Time,"** (chapters 19-22:6). In this section we see symbolic contrast between God's perspective on human history and a humanistic or earthly perspective. The binding of Satan is given in symbol, but in reality it is the victory of resurrection as expressed in Christ.

These sections, with the introduction mentioned, and a fitting conclusion at the end of chapter 22, reveal the basic message of the book. Its symbolic presentations unfold an understanding of history that has its essential strength in the Resurrection.

It is of interest that the last section is the context in which we find the single New Testament presentation of the concept of a millennium. The fact that the millennium concept is in this section suggests to me that the Millennium is referenced to focus on God's purpose beyond time as we know time. This outline is helpful for me in seeking to understand the message of the book of Revelation and in seeing the Millennium to be in some way a celebration of God's purpose beyond "our" time. It appears to be a great celebration of His victory, a celebration in which we will share as He presents the completed kingdom to the Father.

This focuses the millennial reign as a supra-natural celebration, that is, beyond the material order of history as we know it. This involves the world in what the Scripture speaks of as "a new heaven and a new earth." But, on this matter of the meaning of a millennial reign, I recognize a variety of views other than the one I have just stated and they have conditioned my own view in some form.

One view is that of postmillennialism, which holds that the kingdom of God is primarily a present reality and that He will come to earth after the Millennium or one thousand years, is past. Some with this view anticipate the conversion of all the nations as a divine accomplishment prior to the return of Christ, including a long period of earthly peace, with a strong emphasis on the church militant today and triumphant in the future. This is quite optimistic, and would be wonderful, but does not fit my understanding of Scripture.

A second view, and often difficult to distinguish from the preceding, is a-millennialism, holding that there will be no earthly thousand-year reign other than His reign in the church, that Christ's return is imminent, and that the reference to a thousand years is atemporal. The strength of this view is its strong emphasis on the presence and power of the kingdom of grace now, of the reign of Christ in the church, and of the ethic of discipleship in the life of the kingdom as we live now under the rule of Christ. But to me, this view lacks focus on a future "telos" as the expressed victory of our Lord.

A third view is that of pre-millennialism, with several subtypes, holding that, at the second coming of Christ, He will establish an earthly reign, a one thousand year period in which Christ's reign is an actuality for humanity on earth (see George E. Ladd, *The Revelation of Christ's Glory*, p. 14). There are various forms of pre-millennialism, among which the most common distinction is between "classical pre-millennialism" and "dispensational pre-millennialism." Included in the latter form of pre-millennialism are differences of opinion in interpretation regarding a pre-tribulation (the Tribulation being seven years of terrible suffering) rapture, a mid-tribulation rapture, a post-tribulation rapture (rapture meaning a return of Christ for His own) before the coming of the millennial reign of Christ. This view has given rise to the popularized movie, "Left Behind." This emphasis may see His coming as imminent; that it could be at any time, but usually fails to see in periods of great world turmoil what may be the larger meaning of a tribulation in the world.

Such a variety of interpretations makes it evident that biblical studies call us to wait in faith for the return of our Lord and leave the details to His sovereign plan. One person has quipped of holding a pan-millennial view that it will "pan out" all right in the end. (For those interested in further detail, the Baptist theologian Millard Erickson in *Contemporary Options in Eschatology*, offers a fine treatment (pp. 55-181). The biblical emphasis on the return of Christ is a call for us to be watchful and faithful, as anticipating His return affects how we live now.

My own view I call trans-millennialism, (supra-natural or over and beyond this earthly order), being something of a hybrid, agreeing with the pre-millennial that there must be an ultimate "telos" or culmination in victory, and also agreeing in part with the a-millennial, that the rule of God or kingdom is already to be experienced as the reign of Christ. In my view of trans-millennialism, the Millennium is more than expressed in either the pre-millennial or the a-millennial views. It will literally happen just as the resurrection of Christ literally happened, but it need not be of our physical material order just as His resurrection body was not tied to our material order. It will be a celebration, as Tony Compollo says, the coming reign is "party time."

I think my approach is helpful in better understanding the symbolism of the book of Revelation, applicable in John's time to the clash between the church and the Roman Empire but just as (if not even more) applicable in our time, especially in the clash between world religions. It is striking to read the book of the Revelation with careful thought of the related problems of our world as we become a global village: increased population and ethnic wars, problems of world economics and materialism, the clash between the "haves" and the "have nots" and a lack of compassion, increased ethnic violence and moral decadence, tension over weapons of mass destruction, and dangers of world-wide plagues with earthquakes and destructive forces.

In this "end time" as Karl Barth reminds us, we should not overlook the continued presence of the Jewish people as a sermon to the world about belief in Jehovah. Even in their "unbelief" the Jews are a reminder of our Jehovah God. But Jesus helps us distinguish between Old Testament prophecies that were fulfilled in His redemptive role through ministry, death and Resurrection, and prophecies that are focused on His victorious return as risen, exalted Lord. His Word, in prophecies to Israel and to all of us, call for careful interpretation in the context in which we apply them today. Our mission is not to tell Israel that they have a land and future apart from a covenant relation with the Lord. Rather God has called them to faith in Christ, and as Paul says, "and so," (that is, "in this way") all Israel is to be saved (Romans 9:26) and that by the Deliverer who has come out of Zion—Jesus Christ our Lord.

Too many preachers of prophecy are trying to be date-setters by their interpretation of Old Testament prophecies and fail to catch the spirit of Jesus' predictions. We do not know when He will come, but we heed His call to faithfulness and watchfulness. For the Christian, the message remains clear: Jesus is Lord at God's right hand, risen sovereign who will come in power and glory!

Importantly, eschatology does have present implications in calling us to live now in the "escaton" or end time. Living in anticipation of His return brings eschatology—the study of resurrection, death, and judgment—to center stage. We are not dealing with the totally unknown that is yet to happen but with what Jesus has already introduced, which is now extended into the future until its culmination. As stated, history doesn't contain its own fulfillment; rather history is being brought to a culmination already projected in the victory of the exalted Christ. He is Victor. He is Lord. He is our Redeemer and our Sovereign. The Devil is already defeated and we live in the victory of Christ, evil being overcome through the power of Christ until ultimately vanquished by the return of Christ. This we celebrate in faith.

There are some evangelicals who have come to believe that the resurrection is for the saved only, primarily the extension of our lives into a future as the redeemed. That is to say that the lost are resurrected to be judged by God and then to go into eternal destruction and only the redeemed will live. But consider what Jesus said of the lost, "Then they will go away to eternal punishment, but the righteous to eternal life" (Matthew 25:46). Is the eternal punishment annihilation? Paul writes, "He will punish those who do not know God and do not obey the gospel of our Lord Jesus. They will be punished with everlasting destruction and shut out from the presence of the Lord and from the majesty of his power on the day he comes to be glorified in his holy people and to be marveled at among all those who have believed" (2 Thessalonians 1:8-10). The interpretation of this school of thought says that eternal punishment is the eternal loss of existence—being away from God.

The picture of all humanity being resurrected and standing before God in judgment is affirmed in various Scriptures. Daniel writes, "Many of those who sleep in the dust of the earth shall awake, some to everlasting life, and some to shame and everlasting contempt" (Daniel 12:2). This passage, with many of Jesus' statements, and those of Paul to the Thessalonians, (2 Thessalonians 1:8-9), do not suggest annihilation; however they need to be interpreted in relation to the whole scope of scripture and its understanding of our sovereign God.

Paul writes of the time when all persons will come forth from the dead and stand before God. Paul says, "God's righteous judgment will be revealed. For he will repay according to each one's deeds; to those who by patiently doing good seek for glory and honor and immortality, he will give eternal life: while for those who are self-seeking and who obey not the truth but wickedness, there will be wrath and fury. There will be anguish and distress for every one who does evil, the Jew first and also the Greek, but glory and honor and peace for every one who does good, the Jew first and also the Greek. For God shows no partiality" (Romans 2:5-11). Again this same emphasis is expressed in the concluding sections of the book of the Revelation.

"Then I saw a great white throne and the one who sat on it; the earth and the heaven fled from his presence, and no place was found for them. And I saw the dead, great and small, standing before the throne, and books were opened. Also another book was opened, the book of life. And the dead were judged according to their works as recorded in the books. And the sea gave up the dead that were in it. Death and hades gave up the dead that were in them, and all were judged according to what they had done. Then death and hades were thrown into the lake of fire. This is the second death, the lake of fire; and any one whose name was not found written in the book of life was thrown into the lake of fire" (Revelation 20:11-15).

"Then I saw a new heaven and a new earth; for the first heaven and the first earth had passed away and the sea was no more. And I saw the holy city, the New Jerusalem, coming down out of heaven from God, prepared as a bride adorned for her husband. And I heard a loud voice from the throne saying, 'See, the home of God is among mortals. He will dwell with them as their God; and they will be his peoples, and God himself will be with them; he will wipe every tear from their eyes. Death will be no more; mourning and crying and pain will be no more, for the first things have passed away.' And the one who was seated on the throne said, 'See, I am making all things new'" (Revelation 21:1-5). This is our hope!

As stated, we cannot and should not set any dates. Vernard Eller pokes fun at those who want to sell tickets to the battle of Armageddon! In my commentary on Matthew, (*The Communicator's Commentary*), in chapter 24 when Jesus predicted the destruction of Jerusalem, the disciples then asked Him a three-fold question: when shall these things be, what is the sign of Your coming, and what is the sign of the end of the age? Jesus seems to have answered, as I do sometimes in class or seminar, by saying, "I'll take the last question first." He first gave them a review of events that will mark the end of the age (their third question), including the fact that this Gospel will first be preached in the whole world! Then He went back to their first question of the destruction of Jerusalem and described prophetically this event. But when it came to their second question, the sign of His coming, He told them that this time is in the Father's hands, and rather than any indication of a time He gave them instruction on watchfulness. He answered by a remarkable series of parables calling for stewardship (Matthew24:45-51), for our being prepared (Matthew 25:1-13), and a calling to faithfulness (Matthew 25:14-30). He concludes this section with a scene of His coming in judgment, with the emphasis being "in as much as you have done it unto one of the least of these, my brethren, you have done it unto me" (Matthew 25:40). This is our calling, to live and to serve the neighbor in need and to do so in the love of Christ.

With Peter's statements that "God is not willing that any should perish but that all should come to repentance," and that "one day is with the Lord as a thousand years and a thousand years as one day" (2 Peter 3:8-9), it would seem proper to affirm that the God who is dealing with a world of six billion people—most of whom do not know Christ—must not be in a hurry to wrap it up. He may well wait a thousand years! However, "as it was in the day of Noah so shall it be in the coming of the Son of Man." The people at that time had so bound up their society in unbelief that for God to postpone judgment wouldn't have changed things. Just so, it may well be that humanity in our day will tie the world into knots or destroy its very life-sustaining systems that for the Lord to wait longer wouldn't make any real difference to humanity and God can justly bring the end.

Prophecies of conditions that will mark the end times are not to all be interpreted as negative signs. For example "This Gospel shall be preached in all the world and then shall the end come." This is a positive factor. Similarly, in this day of the global village and the need for mutuality in helping the needy, predictions of a global economy may be meant as positive and not negative, although idolizing this as our security would be heretical. These are some of my current reflections as I seek to be watchful in expectation of His coming.

Our eschatological hope includes of course our own resurrection from the dead and our sharing the ages of the ages with our Lord. Since, with Dr. Newbigin, I hold that "Resurrection does not fit into any other world view" I must say that resurrection is its own claim, the word of a new reality with which God has confronted us. In this day of post-enlightenment and post-modernity we need to witness to our faith, standing in this reality. This is not escapism but what I call a Christological realism as our view of life. Our witness is not merely one of words, of philosophical argument, but of the new life known and shown by sharing His Resurrection.

The quality of the new life for the disciple is grounded in a faith relationship with the risen Christ. This identity is with the same Jesus who, living among humanity, taught and lived the will of God. His Resurrection is the divine answer to the redemptive engagement that cost Jesus His life. Here is the full word of overcoming evil with good. Between violence on the one hand and appeasement on the other, there is a third way—the way of agape, self-giving love. This calls for active and creative ways of helping people and investing in such programs as minister to human need. And why not, rather than investing in military equipment? National policy could be changed to something far more neighborly and constructive in the global community. The dynamic of this love is its power to change lives in relationship. The cost of this love is that it may lead to a cross. As we live by His self-giving love, the witness will be felt in our compassion, in our actions of faith, until people will say again, "Behold, how they love one another." Jesus said, "By this shall all people know that you are my disciples, if you have love one to another" (John 13:35).

In our studies of futurism, anticipating the changes that will meet us in this 21st century, we need the resources of this Resurrection hope. We need to experience the reconciliation with our neighbors, which is possible by God's grace. We have become not only a world community but also a one-world house. With modern communication, the globe is being brought together in one context. The majority of the world's population now lives in cities, and the privileges and the problems of urbanization increases the need for us to understand the way of peace and reconciliation (see Ray Bakke on the Urban Church).

The deprivations and hunger of two-thirds of the world increases the call to stewardship and distribution and calls for a spirit of unselfishness that is anxious to share with the needy. The pluralism of our society with the increase of religious dialogue, as each group wrestles with the problems that confront us, calls for more understanding and clarity in our sharing of the message of Christ. With half of the world's population under the age of twenty, we are called to provide education in moral and spiritual matters as well as technological and scientific matters— if we are to prepare competent leaders and communities for the future. The exploitation of natural resources calls for more concern for preservation of resources for the generations to come. How wonderful it would be if our government would hear the Christian witness to be a call for more international aid to the needy in food, medicine, education, etc. The words from Jesus' parable take on a very immediate urgency, "Occupy until I come" (Luke 19:13).

The church, if it keeps itself free from any one culture or nationalism, can move throughout the world in a freedom to introduce people to Christ in their own context. It is the mission of all Christians to interpret the meaning of discipleship in the world today by love and service and with its moral and social dimensions, all of which are enriched by our understanding of the lordship of Christ in the kingdom of God.

Dr. James McClendon sees us as having three different ways in which we work at interpreting life: we are (1) part of the natural order; (2) part of a social world; and (3) part of an eschatological realm, the kingdom of God. His conclusion is that "As witnesses to the resurrection of Jesus Christ from the dead we live in the presence of One who makes all things new by his Spirit," (p. 66). We are participants in a new order, bearers of a new life, members of a redeemed community living under the lordship of the exalted Christ!

Our resurrection future brings a message to the church in the present. Hauerwas and Willimon's *Resident Aliens*, in describing the church as resident aliens, calls us to the awareness that "Each age must come, fresh and new, to the realization that God, not nations, rules the world." And further, "We would like a church that again asserts that God, not nations, rules the world, that the boundaries of God's kingdom transcend those of Caesar and that the main political task of the church is the formation of people who see clearly the cost of discipleship and are willing to pay the price" (pp. 28, 48). For those who seek to follow Christ, there is both challenge and affirmation: to be faithful. Our God is faithful.

The Resurrection means that God has already made history come out right in terms of making clear the divine goal. His victory is the way in which things as we see them will end! Christianity is not a head-trip; it is walking with Jesus in the community of disciples, sharing in His eschatological victory as present reality. Faith is to live in the freedom and power of grace, being transformed into the likeness of Christ. By the victory of Christ and His sovereign rule as resurrected Lord, we are created a new people in the world. In our communities of faith, we are given by God as "light in the world," as "salt to the earth." Even society is made better because of the presence of the church. We believe the resurrection of Jesus Christ is the decisive act of God, which has ever since been pivotal for Christian belief and Christian moral life.

We believe in the return of Christ as interfaced with our believing in the resurrection of Christ. But it must be asked, can we grasp, *do* we grasp, the stupendous impact of resurrection realities?

Let me summarize a number of realities that Resurrection conveys. His Resurrection means:

♦ He is who He said, the actual Son of God. Whether we have been inclined to do Christology from above as the given of Scriptural doctrine, or Christology from below as emerging from our study of the man Jesus, the fact is that we now do Christology from the Resurrection (Acts 2:32-33).

♦ His death was not a defeat but a declaration of God's reconciling love in the face of evil's most intense hostility—"he bore our sins in his own body on the cross" (1 Peter 2:24).

♦ His life and death are together given extended meaning, for the resurrected Lord is the same Jesus who lived and taught the will of God hence His earthly ministry is verified and extended as God's Word to us.

♦ Now we interpret God's actions and words in all of history by and through the person and work of the living Jesus Christ.

♦ He is head of a new community, a redeemed people, a reconciled people called the church, and that His primary work in the world now is through the redeemed community that He is continually creating.

♦ As He promised, He gives the Holy Spirit to be His sovereign presence to guide and enrich the lives of those who join in solidarity with Him!

♦ He now imparts this same resurrection power to us. As His disciples, we are enabled by the Holy Spirit to live in a positive lifestyle that transcends the death-dealing levels of sin. His Resurrection releases us from the perversions of self-centeredness by the dynamic of God-centeredness infused into our lives by the Holy Spirit.

♦ He carries on His work of redeeming humanity by His unconditional love and He extends this by and through the lives of His disciples in every age, in every culture, race, and nationality.

♦ Through the church, He confronts societies and governments with a new quality of community, and the presence of this community calls them to something better even in their unbelief.

♦ These communities of freedom in grace are enabled by His Resurrection power to overcome evil with good, sharing with God in His sovereign self-determining ministry of reconciliation.

♦ He will complete His mission, complete His kingdom, and will then turn the kingdom over to the Father.

♦ He will come again to call all humanity to its account, for He is at God's right hand and "From thence he shall come to judge the living and the dead" (*Apostles' Creed;* Ephesians 1:20-22)

♦ In His acts to conclude history as we know it, He will welcome His disciples into the eternal glory, "And so shall we ever be with the Lord" (1 Thessalonians 4:17).

The membership covenant that we adopted at the Washington Community Fellowship, D.C., did not focus on the differences of millennial views, but on the fellowship of hope in which we share. The tenth and final point reads simply: "We believe in the personal return of our Lord Jesus Christ, and emphasize the victory of the risen Christ and anticipate joyously His coming!"

"May the God of peace, who through the blood of the eternal covenant brought back from the dead our Lord Jesus, that great Shepherd of the sheep, equip you with everything good for doing his will, and may he work in us what is pleasing to Him, through Jesus Christ, to whom be glory for ever and ever. Amen" (Hebrews 13:20-21).

BIBLIOGRAPHY

AUGSBURGER, MYRON S.,
Principles of Biblical Interpretation in Mennonite Theology, Herald Press, 1967
The Communicator's Commentary, Matthew, Word, 1982
Walking in the Resurrection, Herald Press, 1976

AULEN, GUSTAF,
Christus Victor, S.P.C.K., 1950

BAILLIE, DONALD M.,
God was in Christ, Charles Scribner, 1948

BARTH, KARL,
A Shorter Commentary on Romans, John Knox, 1959
Dogmatics in Outline, SCM, 1949

BARTH, MARKUS,
Justification, Eerdmans, 1971

BARTH, MARKUS, AND FLETCHER, VERNE H.,
Acquittal by Resurrection, Holt, Rinehart and Winston, 1964

BENDER, HAROLD S.,
Conrad Grebel, Founder of the Swiss Brethren, Goshen, IN, 1950

BOCKMUEHL, KLAUS E.,
The Unreal God, Helmers & Howard, 1988

BONHOEFFER, DIETRICH,
The Cost of Discipleship, Macmillan, 1951

BOSCH, DAVID J.,
A Spirituality of the Road, Herald Press, 1979

BRUNNER, EMIL,
Letter to the Romans

CULLMAN, OSCAR,
Christ and Time, Westminster, Philadelphia, PA, 1950

DENNEY, JAMES,
Death of Christ, Tyndale Edition, 1951

DRIVER, JOHN,
Understanding the Atonement, Herald Press, 1986

DUPRE, LOUIS, AND SALIERS, DON E.,
Christian Spirituality, Post Reformation and Modern, Crossroad, NY,
1989

ELLER, VERNERD,
The Most Revealing Book of the Bible, Eerdmans, 1974

ELLUL, JACQUES,
The Ethics of Freedom, Eerdmans, 1976
The Subversion of Christianity, Eerdmans, 1986

ERB, PAUL,
Bible Prophecy, Questions and Answers, Herald Press, 1978

ERICKSON, MILLARD J.,
Contemporary Options in Eschatology, Baker Book House, 1977

EWERT, DAVID,
And Then Comes the End, Herald Press, 1980

FILSON, FLOYD,
Jesus Christ the Risen Lord, Abingdon, 1956

FORSYTH, P.T.,
The Work of Christ, London, Hodder and Stoughton, 1910

FINGER, THOMAS N.,
Christian Theology, an Eschatological Approach, 2 Volume, Thomas Nelson, Herald Press, 1985 and 1989

GEORGE, TIMOTHY,
Theology of the Reformers, Broadman, 1988

GREATHOUSE, WILLIAM M.,
From the Apostles to Wesley, Beacon Press, 1981

GREEN, MICHAEL,
The Empty Cross of Jesus, 1985

HAUERWAS, STANLEY,
A Community of Character, University of Notre Dame Press, 1981

HAUERWAS, STANLEY AND WILLIMON, WILLIAM H.,
Resident Aliens, Abingdon, 1990

HAYS, RICHARD B.,
The Moral Vision of the New Testament, Harper Collins, 1996

HERSHBERGER, GUY F., Ed.
The Recovery of the Anabaptist Vision, Herald Press, 1957

KLASSEN, WALTER,
Anabaptism: Neither Catholic nor Protestant, Conrad Press, 1981

KRAUS, NORMAN,
Jesus Christ Our Lord, Herald Press, 1987

LINTS, RICHARD,
The Fabric of Theology, Eerdmans, 1993

MACKINTOSH, H.R.,
The Christian Experience of Forgiveness, London, Nisbit, 1927

MCCLENDON, JAMES,
Ethics: Systematic Theology Ethics, Volume 1, Abingdon, Nashville, 1986

MCGRATH, ALISTER E.,
Understanding Jesus, Zondervan, 1987

MOLTMANN, JURGEN,
Following Jesus Christ in the World Today, Institute of Mennonite Studies, Occ. Papers, No.4, 1983
Theology of Hope, 1967
The Crucified God, Harper, 1974

MUMAW, JOHN R.,
The Ressurection, Herald Press, 1963

MOUNCE, ROBERT,
The Book of Revelation, The New International Commentary of the New Testament, Eerdmans, 1977

NEILL, STEPHEN,
Jesus Through Many Eyes, Fortress, 1976

NEWBIGIN, LESSLIE,
Foolishness to the Greeks, Eerdmans, 1986

O'DONOVAN, OLIVER,
Resurrection and Moral Order, Eerdmans, 1986

PANNENBURG, WOLFHART,
Jesus-God and Man, Westminster, 1977
Systematic Theology, Volume I, Eerdmans, 1991

RICHARDSON, ALAN,
An Introduction to the Theology of the New Testament, Harper and Row, 1954

SCHAFFER, FRANCIS A.,
The God Who Is There, IVP, 1968

SCHILLEBEECKX, EDWARD,
Jesus and Experiment in Christology, Crossroad, 1981

SINE, TOM,
Wild Hope, Word Publishing, 1991

SNYDER, C. ARNOLD,
The Life and Thought of Michael Sattler, Herald Press, 1984

SOBRINO, JON,
Christology at the Crossroads, Orbis, 1979

STOTT, JOHN R.W.,
Romans, God's Good News for the World, IVP, 1994
The Cross of Christ, IVP, 1986
Evangelical Truth, IVP, 1999

SWARTLEY, WILLARD,
Slavery, Sabbath, War, and Women, Herald Press, 1983

TENNEY, MERRILL,
Resurrection Realities, Harper and Row, 1963

VOLF, MIROSLAV,
Exclusion and Embrace, Abingdon, 1996

WEAVER, J. DENNY,
The Nonviolent Atonement, Eerdmans, 2001

WEBSTER, DOUGLAS,
A Passion for Christ, Zondervan, 1987

WENGER, J.C.,
Christ the Redeemer and Judge, Herald Press, 1942

YODER, JOHN H.,
Preface to Theology-Christology and Theological Method, AMBS, 1981
The Politics of Jesus, Eerdmans, 1972